The Legends of Derby County

The Legends of Derby County

IAN HALL

breedon **books**
PUBLISHING

First published in Great Britain in 2001 by
The Breedon Books Publishing Company Limited
Breedon House, 3 The Parker Centre, Derby, DE21 4SZ.

Photographs have been supplied by Colorsport, Empics and Raymond's News Agency.

ISBN 1 85983 246 6

Printed and bound by Butler & Tanner Lrd, Frome, Somerset
Jacket printing by GreenShires Ltd, Leicester

Contents

Introduction 7

Aljosa Asanovic – a little bit of mystery 9

Dai Astley – punch *and* craft 11

Jack Barker – masterly and hard 13

Geoff Barrowcliffe - a footballing full-back 15

Harry Bedford - one of the great goalscorers 17

Steve Bloomer – personality in every action 19

Colin Boulton – a long apprenticeship 21

Jack Bowers – everything a striker should be 23

Steve Buckley – calm authority 25

Jimmy Bullions – the modest Cup winner 27

Horacio Carbonari – good feet for a big lad 29

Willie Carlin – marvellous wee footballer 31

Raich Carter – immense self belief 33

Brian Clough – he took the breath away 35

George Collin – he stopped the others 37

Tommy Cooper – polished and poised 39

Arthur Cox – individually and collectively 41

Sammy Crooks – just a lovely bloke 43

Bill Curry – he loved scoring goals 45

Peter Daniel – the quiet man 47

Glyn Davies – up and at 'em 49

Roger Davies – awkward to play against 51

Bobby Davison – sharp as a tack 53

Peter Doherty – rebel with a cause 55

Dally Duncan – wonderful left foot 57

Alan Durban – always there 59

Stefano Eranio – sheer quality 61

Marco Gabbiadini – an enigma 63

Hughie Gallacher – could make a ball talk 65

Archie Gemmill – he was everywhere 67

Charlie George – he just hit it 69

Archie Goodall – footballer and showman 71

John Goodall – Nature's gentleman 73

Les Green – agile, athletic, strong 75

John Gregory – dictated the game 77

Reg Harrison – always laughing 79

Kevin Hector – that little bit extra 81

Terry Hennessey – he played against Pele 83

Rob Hindmarch – a natural defender 85

Alan Hinton – a different kind of courage 87

Jack Howe – a rarity in football 89

Gordon Hughes – enthusiasm and energy 91

George Jobey – he knew his football 93

Errington Keen – a step too far? 95

Francis Lee – supremely confident 97

Jack Lee – another England striker 99

Leon Leuty – the best of all? 101

Martin McDonnell – enjoyed a sliding tackle 103

Roy McFarland – good enough for any team 105

John McGovern – a knitter-together 107

Paul McGrath – life in the old dog 109

Johnny McIntyre – a love of football 111

Dave Mackay – already a legend 113

Stuart McMillan – Cup Final manager 115

Ted McMinn – the Tin Man 117

Reg Matthews – what a repertoire! 119

Albert Mays – that back pass! 121

Jimmy Methven – player and manager 123

Garry Micklewhite – multi-purpose footballer 125

Johnny Morris – he wriggled and slithered 127

Bert Mozley – football was fun 129

Chick Musson – is he playing today? 131

Henry Newton – high cruising speed 133

Jack Nicholas – the man who lifted the Cup 135

David Nish – he had time 137

John O'Hare – a great target man 139

Ken Oxford – an old-fashioned goalkeeper 141

Jack Parry joker in the pack 143

Mart Poom – how many points is he worth? 145

Steve Powell – he was just brilliant 147

Tommy Powell – charmed us all 149

Jesse Pye – he had a few tricks 151

Peter Ramage – never stopped running 153

Fabrizio Ravanelli – all the credentials 155

Bruce Rioch – no frills and powerful 157

Reg Ryan – shrewd tactician 159

Dean Saunders – balance, agility, fitness 161

Peter Shilton – mistakes were so rare 163

Jim Smith – a great personality 165

Jack Stamps – a lion of a man 167

Billy Steel – you couldn't play with him 169

George Stephenson – neat and clever 171

Igor Stimac – he lit the spark 173

Harry Storer – a spade was a shovel 175

Ray Straw – local boy made good 177

Peter Taylor – the straight man 179

George Thornewell – flying right winger 181

Colin Todd – style and panache 183

Frank Upton – strong men flinched 185

Robbie van der Laan – a great talker 187

Paulo Wanchope – so unpredictable 189

Tim Ward – the gentleman footballer 191

Ben Warren – he always came home 193

Ron Webster – he knew his business 195

Jackie Whitehouse – inspiration to his colleagues . .197

George Williams – the powerful engine 199

Kevin Wilson – managers valued him 201

Vic Woodley – retirement to a Cup Final 203

Mark Wright – nothing he couldn't do 205

Ray Young – compared to a great player 207

Bibliography 208

"There are some things wrong with clubs, with managers, with administrators, with Pressmen, with referees. The only thing with which there is nothing wrong, is the game itself."

Joe Mercer

Introduction

IT seems like a long time ago, then again, like yesterday, since Derby County played at The Baseball Ground. I don't mean the emasculated, all-seater Baseball Ground, with an attendance limit of 17,000 and neat rows of plastic seats.What I mean is the all-singing, all-swaying Baseball Ground of clear floodlit nights and dull, grey, rainswept afternoons. With a nip of frost in the air at night, or in the afternoons, a swirl of smoke from Ley's Castings, drifting over the Offilers Ales shed roof on the Pop side and across the muddy apology of a pitch. Ah, yes, the pitch. Like a combination of quicksand and treacle, it drew the last remnants of energy from tired limbs, like a dentist drawing teeth. It squelched in winter and dried rock hard in spring and defeated the best efforts of a succession of groundsmen for a hundred years to prepare a surface to match the standard of some of the great players who played on it. Like grandma's bread and drippin', the Baseball Ground and that pitch were inseparable.

Then came Pride Park. A modern high technological stadium with pristine facilities, corporate logos and all the expectations of the 21st century. Electric trolleys to ferry the less able – and some, able – from the South Car Park, to an entrance more like Grand Central Station, or a five-star hotel. Restaurants, banqueting suites, the Queen visiting regularly and a full international match on a balmy spring evening. And of course, the pitch. Green, lush like velvet, even at the end of a season. Such a pitch brings tears to the eyes of former players. The aches and pains of another era fade to a memory, at the sight of this pitch.

Never forget the pitch. It starts there and ends there, this football business. The triumphs, disasters, heartaches and joys in football begin on the pitch. Everything in football stems from there, legends are created...

Aljosa Asanovic – a little bit of mystery

IT would be hard to find a player who raised the profile of a football club more than Aljosa Asanovic. His coming to Derby County, in the summer of 1996, showed the football world that the club was not just content to get into the Premier League to make up the numbers. For Asanovic had been one of the stars of a very good Croatian team that had surprised many with the quality of its football in Euro '96. After the tournament, several clubs would have been prepared to pay big money to sign Asanovic, but they were unable to do so. On the advice of Igor Stimac and before the tournament began, Jim Smith had already signed him from Hadjuk Split, for £900,000. When the tournament ended, Asanovic was a star.

Asanovic added style, class and reputation to the Rams' midfield. Tall, dark, with a long rangy stride, Asanovic's left foot could produce moments of intricate magic and, occasionally, ferocious power. Those who were there will never forget the explosive free-kick at Stamford Bridge, when from at least 35 yards, he let fly and left the Chelsea goalkeeper and the home crowd completely stunned. More often, though, he was to be seen in the throes of shaking off a defender, or two, or three, before releasing a pass to a teammate in a bit of space. More space than the colleague might have bargained for, because Asanovic was happy to attract the opposition to him like flies round a honey pot. Not that he was behind the door in the pushing, pulling, shirt holding and falling over stakes. Sojourns around different countries in Europe had taught him a few tricks. An ability to win dubious free-kicks from naive referees was also a favoured tactic, together with an air of complete innocence when the decision went his way. Conversely, there was much tossing of the head and a waves of annoyance when the official rumbled his ploy.

Off the field, he tended to keep himself to himself. He wore smallish rimmed spectacles which gave him the studious air of a lawyer, or an accountant, and for quite a while it was thought his command of the English language was poor. In fact, it was better than he made out, but like many things, there was a little bit of mystery about Asanovic.

Asanovic played 37 Premiership matches, plus one substitute appearance, for Derby County, but after an excellent first half-season which did much to establish the Rams in the Premier League, one felt he became increasingly unhappy with the way the management expected him to play, often wide out on the left rather than in a central role to which his talents seemed more suited. He was transferred to Italian club Napoli in December 1997 and later played in Greece for Panathinaikos.

In a brief period, Asanovic did well for Derby County. He had the confidence of an established international player and was an automatic selection for Croatia when that country was a force in international football. He was, though, somewhat of a loose cannon and one of the increasing number of football bounty hunters who trek around Europe. Teams cannot be built around such nomads. Asanovic was like the brandy sauce on the Christmas pudding, rather than the pudding itself – but it tasted good while it lasted.

Dai Astley – punch *and* craft

'A CENTRE-FORWARD with punch AND craft. How many clubs would clearly like one now? Someone who could start a move inside his own half and be up in the opponents' penalty area to finish it off only a few moments later! Such a player was Dai Astley, who joined the Rams from Aston Villa on 12 November 1936.' So said the *Derby County Supporters' Association Year Book* for 1960-61, looking back at some of the club's greatest stars.

Harry Bedford, Jack Bowers and Hughie Gallacher were centre-forwards who immediately preceded Dai Astley in the Derby County attack and they were hard acts to follow. Some thought impossible, but Astley made a pretty good job of doing so. He had a good pedigree. He was a schoolboy international for Wales and on leaving school, went to be a miner. He played for Merthyr Town, then in the Third Division South, and then joined Charlton Athletic, also in the Southern Section, before being transferred to First Division Aston Villa in 1931. At Villa Park his scoring record of 100 goals in 170 League and Cup appearances kept him well in the public eye, but despite his goals he couldn't prevent Aston Villa being relegated for the first time in their history and he asked for a transfer. Rams manager George Jobey had to move quicky to secure yet another international centre-forward in November 1936.

Tall and quite slim, Astley was not as strong or powerful as Bowers, nor was he as skilful as Gallacher, but he was a useful footballer and could score goals. In 27 League matches in his first season at the Baseball Ground, he scored 25 goals, including three hat-tricks, as Derby County finished fourth in Division One. Added to the goals he had scored for Aston Villa earlier and including FA Cup goals, his season's tally was 34. The following season he was an ever-present and scored 17 goals. He always appreciated the service he received from wingers Sammy Crooks and Dally Duncan. In 1984 he recalled, "Dally or Sammy used to sort of pinpoint where they were going to cross the ball and I must have scored a terrific amount with my head at Derby, more than anywhere, because for the majority of crosses I could just stand in the middle and head them in. Dally or Sammy often said, 'You want 'em in the middle, you'll have them in the middle. You stay there, I'll do the work.' And that was it. Who could argue with that?"

In season 1938-39, Astley moved to inside-right, to accommodate Dave McCulloch at centre-forward. McCulloch was a Scottish international and another Jobey signing, but the move wasn't successful and Astley's goalscoring ratio declined considerably. Nevertheless, it was a surprise when he was somewhat reluctantly transferred to Blackpool in January 1939. In May of that year he was again capped by Wales, against France in Paris, thus achieving the distinction of winning international caps with four different clubs: Charlton Athletic (1), Aston Villa (9), Derby County (2) and Blackpool.

After the war, Astley played for a short time in France before embarking on a coaching career that took him around the world, to places like Persia, Sweden and Italy. He was coach to Inter-Milan and Sampdoria and then the Danish club Djurgårdens before returning to live and work in Derby in the 1950s. For a time he and his wife lived in Green Lane before they retired to live at Birchington, near Margate, where Dai Astley died in November 1989.

Jack Barker – masterly and hard

GREAT centre-halves have featured strongly in Derby County's history. Jack Barker was one of those. Many older supporters who saw him play claim he was the best of all. Archie Goodall, Leon Leuty, Roy McFarland, Mark Wright, Igor Stimac, Horacio Carbonari, the list is formidable and Rams' legend Tommy Powell saw all except Goodall play. "You're talking about different eras, but I think Jack Barker was, probably, the best centre-half I've ever seen. He could mix it and he could bring it down on his chest and send it this way and that, no problem, right foot, or left, sweet as a nut. I wouldn't say he was blessed with terrific speed, or anything like that, but he wasn't slow. He was masterly."

Broadcaster and local historian Roy Christian watched from the terraces. "He was a good defender as well, but what I remember were those lovely passes he gave out to the wings. Like Carbonari, who is good at that too. He had good ball control. Centre-halves weren't always good footballers, but he was and he was a very tough defender. I wouldn't say he was dirty, but he was very hard."

Alf Jeffries played with him: "Of course you can only talk about the era he played in – the ball was different, the rules were different, pitches were different – but I reckon Jack Barker was really one of the best centre-halves I've ever seen." Jeffries also saw another side to Barker, which perhaps did him no favours when he later became, briefly, a rather unsuccessful manager of Derby County; Jack Barker was no diplomat. "Jack's trouble was his mouth, you see. That was Jack's trouble, otherwise he'd have got more England caps. He couldn't hold his tongue with the powers-that-be. He was a lad, but he was a good player. A tough sod, he was. He came out of the pits, did Jack Barker."

Indeed, he once survived a pit disaster and when former Derby player Ivan Sharpe, by then a distinguished journalist, asked him if he would be worried by the Hampden Roar, Barker replied, "I've heard far worse than that – the roar of a pit falling in."

George Jobey signed Barker and Jack Bowers as youngsters in May 1928, from Midland League clubs Denaby United and Scunthorpe United respectively. Both Barker and Bowers were christened John William and both went on to play for England, one at centre-half and one at centre-forward. Barker played 11 times for his country and captained England in his final international match, against Wales in 1937. For much of his second season at Derby he was pushed into the background by Tommy Davison, but after that he played throughout the 1930s in what was one of the most successful periods in Derby County's history. He took over the captaincy when Tommy Cooper was transferred to Liverpool in 1934 and his total appearances for the Rams numbered 353.

Barker played at a time when football was changing. The offside law was altered in 1925 and Arsenal were one of the first to restrict the attacking advances of the old-style centre-half to a more defensive role. They had much success and became the outstanding team of the 1930s with this method. Other clubs followed suit and Barker found that the style he had developed as a boy, under the older pattern of play, needed modification. He still attacked when possible but it was sometimes thought he overdid it and eventually, England turned to a more defence-minded stopper in Alf Young of Huddersfield Town. Perhaps, too, at Derby, Barker's penchant for attack cost the club the top honours in the game. Nevertheless, the Rams were always an attractive side to watch and the record attendances they established at several Division One grounds bears testament to George Jobey and Jack Barker's philosophy. In any case, Barker was unlikely to change. He died in Derby in January 1982.

Geoff Barrowcliffe - a footballing full-back

GEOFF Barrowcliffe was one of the most accomplished full-backs I have ever seen. He was good enough to play at centre-forward and did a serviceable job in other positions as well, but it was at full-back where he made most of his 475 League appearances for Derby County. Only seven players in the club's history have passed 500 appearances in total for the Rams, and Barrowcliffe's 503 appearances overall puts him in that very select category.

Barrowcliffe was a footballing full-back. His ball control was better than most midfield players and his passing, long and short, was very accurate. Moreover, the timing of his passing was so good. You were rarely conscious of receiving a difficult ball from Barrowcliffe, or one which put you in trouble. Playing in front of him was a delight. He did have his critics. Some said that fast wingers gave him trouble, others found fault with his tackling, but despite a period when Harry Storer signed the quicker and tougher-tackling Tony Conwell to replace him for a while, Barrowcliffe held off all-comers. The number of appearances, for his only club, speak for themselves.

There can be little doubt that had Barrowcliffe been transferred to a top club, he might well have played for England. Reg Ryan, himself an Irish international and Derby County's inspirational captain in the middle 1950s, was in no doubt, but if Barrowcliffe ever had any ambitions in that direction, it wasn't apparent. Born and bred in Ilkeston, he was happy to play for his local club and the close friendships he retained with playing colleagues, throughout his career and beyond, bore testament to the regard and affection in which he was held. A more genuine and honest individual never played football – except when pork pie was at stake.

For some unearthly reason, in the late 1950s and early 1960s, a plate of pork pie was usually placed in the dressing-room after a match. Barrowcliffe was always the quickest to get dressed after a game and, in any case, he had to catch the 5.05pm train from Friar Gate station back to Ilkeston. George Darwin was one who did fancy a bit of pork pie, but he began to find his little treat hard to come by, as it kept disappearing before he could get his hands on any. Eventually, he realised that the most likely culprit was a certain individual who used to dash into the bath, dress like lightning and was on his way down Osmaston Road before he, George, had recovered from the second half. It all led to an unholy row one Monday morning, after the 'phantom pie snatcher' had struck again on the previous Saturday. After that, a few pieces of pork pie began to be left on the plate. To this day, Geoff Barrowcliffe denies culpability.

Barrowcliffe continued playing after he finished with League football. He coached and managed locally, for Heanor Town, Moorgreen Colliery, Long Eaton United, Kimberley Town, Radford and Rolls-Royce. On one occasion he was uncharacteristically slightly late to play for the ex-Rams team in a charity match on a Sunday afternoon. He explained that he usually turned out on a Sunday morning for his son's pub team and he'd come straight from playing in such a match. He then turned out again, to give another of his usual immaculate performances, playing the full 90 minutes in heavy conditions. He was 63 years old!

Harry Bedford – one of the great goalscorers

HARRY Bedford was born at Calow near Chesterfield and became one of the great goalscorers of English football. In 486 appearances he scored 308 goals, including 152 goals in 218 appearances for Derby County. Eventually, he was superseded at the beginning of the 1930s by another great goalscorer, Jack Bowers, who was even more prolific than Bedford.

Bedford was signed by George Jobey from Blackpool, in 1925 for £3,250, after beginning his career on the books of Nottingham Forest just after World War One. He'd already scored 112 League goals for Blackpool and had played for England twice. When he got to Derby he continued the trend by scoring 27 League goals in his first season. He was Derby County's leading scorer for five successive seasons and in 1929-30 equalled the previous record held by Alf Bentley of 30 League goals in a season. In League matches alone he scored 142 goals in 203 matches, an impressive average of 0.7 goals per match. He scored four goals in a match on three occasions and only Steve Bloomer, with 14, bettered his total of ten hat-tricks.

According to local historian and broadcaster, Roy Christian, Bedford was a strongly-built, bustling type of centre-forward, quite good in the air and not without skill on the floor, but he was more deliberate than quick and owed much of his scoring ability to a keen positional sense in crowded goalmouths. He had a slightly receding hairline and a glowering countenance, which persuaded opponents he was not a player to be meddled with and, like all goalscorers, he had plenty of courage.

Derby County were in Division Two when Bedford joined them, but promotion was achieved in his first season and by the time he left to join Newcastle United, for £4,000 in December 1930, the Rams were an established Division One side, having been runners-up in 1929-30. The emergence of Jack Bowers meant that Bedford played a number of matches at inside-right, where he played alongside right winger Sammy Crooks, who often referred to him as being one of the best partners he ever had.

About that time a common theme emerged. Supporters were critical of the club's policy of keeping a tight grip on financial affairs and with Bowers scoring freely, no doubt manager Jobey had an eye on the transfer fee. Whatever the reason for Bedford's move, Derby County went on to become a team which consistently finished towards the top of Division One during the 1930s. Bedford, himself, topped the Newcastle scoring list in his first season at St James' Park. Everyone benefited.

After two years at Newcastle, Bedford was transferred to Sunderland – unusual in those days for a player to play for those two rival clubs – and Bradford (Park Avenue) before going to play for Chesterfield, his home-town club. In 1937, after a spell as player-coach with Heanor Town, he returned briefly to Newcastle, as trainer, before taking up a post in Derby with the Rolls-Royce Fire Service and he was also masseur to Derbyshire County Cricket Club for a period. During the 1950s he managed both Belper Town and Heanor Town and later became a scout for Arsenal. He died in Derby in June 1976.

Steve Bloomer – personality in every action

A BLACK and white marble plinth and plaque in memory of Steve Bloomer was unveiled in 1998. It stands in Derby's Lock-Up Yard as a permanent reminder of Derby County's greatest player: 525 appearances; 332 goals in a career that lasted from 1892 to 1914; 28 goals in 21 England appearances; Derby's leading League scorer for 13 successive seasons and 15 overall. The following is an extract from *Association Football and the Men Who Made It* edited by Alfred Gibson and William Pickford and published in 1906.

'Picture to yourself a slight, pale-faced indolent looking lad, strolling on to the field in a casual manner, and you have a fair impression of Stephen Bloomer, one of the greatest forwards who ever played for England. A more unlikely looking athlete one would scarce select as as a great football player. Of physique, in the general sense, he has none. He looks more like a man who would break down in the first ten minutes than one who would last the full hour and a half in a scorching Cup tie or an International match. He is not the sort of man whose life any doctor would insure at sight, although if the truth were known he is sound as a bell, possessed of a blacksmith's lungs and a four-cylinder heart warranted to work in any climate.

'In his style of play he is also unlike any great forward of our time. The aim and end of football is to get goals, and Bloomer will not be a party to mere finesse. Embroidery and fancy work he leaves to the artists who like that sort of thing. He is possessed with the one grand idea – to get goals, and to get them with the least possible expenditure of time and energy.

'There is only one Bloomer, and his methods are his own; his style is unique. To watch him on the field in repose one could hardly imagine or guess at the gifts and graces of this man, but to see him in action is to see a figure full of fire and brimming vitality that stamps personality on every action. He does nothing like anyone else. That dash for the goal-line is a Bloomer dash; that single-handed dribble a Bloomer dribble; that fierce rattling shot is a Bloomer shot; that superb forward pass is a Bloomer pass; that glorious bid for victory in the 11th hour is the consummation of Bloomer's art. He has made himself the power he is and has been by reason of an irrepressible audacity, an irresistible desire to conquer, which intense vitality often brings with it.

'This triumph of the strong will, those ruling passions, have made Bloomer so great a footballer. He is a strange compound of the stoic and the philosopher. He gives the spectator the impression of being unnaturally calm. As he stands hand on hip one might imagine he had no interest in the game. If the ball is not in his vicinity he looks on in languid interest. But see him 'on the ball', and his whole attitude and features become transformed. he is then a man of action, a living force, a strong, relentless, destroying angel'.

Steve Bloomer retired as a player in 1914 and with less then impeccable timing went to coach in Germany not long before war was declared. He was interned for the duration and afterwards coached in Spain – taking his club to a Spanish Cup Final victory over Real Madrid – and Holland before working at the Baseball Ground, latterly as a 'general assistant'. In 1938 his health was failing and a public subscription sent him on a cruise. Three weeks after his return he was dead. The streets of Derby were packed as his cortège passed by.

Certainly Steve Bloomer could be called football's first superstar. His face advertised football boots and tonic in an age before radio and television. When the *Queen Mary* made her maiden voyage, his image was aboard, part of a mural of famous Englishmen. And even in 2001, his name still echoes around Pride Park when the specially-written club 'anthem' is played over the loudspeakers. Legends don't come any larger.

Colin Boulton – a long apprenticeship

THERE have been two goalkeepers called Boulton in Derby County's history. They were not related. Frank Boulton missed the 1946 FA Cup Final because of injury. Colin Boulton played in every match in both of Derby County's championship triumphs in the early 1970s, the only player to do so. Lady Luck can be fickle with the goalkeeping fraternity.

Not that things came easily to Colin Boulton. He was training as a police cadet in his home town of Cheltenham when Tim Ward signed him as a 19-year-old in August 1964, recommended by another young Derby player from Cheltenham, Nigel Cleevely. Reg Matthews was still the number-one at Derby but when he was injured late that 1964-65 season, Boulton played the last half dozen games, starting with a 3-0 home defeat by Newcastle. One draw, five defeats and 17 goals conceded was not an auspicious start for the young goalkeeper as the Rams finished ninth in Division Two. Matthews recovered and was an ever-present the following season. By January 1967 he had completed a run of 70 consecutive League matches and Boulton was confined to the reserve team. Then injury struck again. Boulton was recalled for an FA Cup tie at Norwich in January 1967. The Rams lost 3-0. Still Boulton had not been on a winning side. Three League games followed, two defeats and a draw, before finally, in his 11th appearance, spread over two and a half seasons, Boulton finished on the winning side, as the Rams beat Bury 3-0 at the Baseball Ground. He made a total of 14 League appearances that season, but when Brian Clough took over as manager in the close season, Matthews was back again. Boulton made only five appearances in 1967-68, but hope was rekindled when Matthews retired in the summer. It looked like Boulton's big opportunity had arrived. It hadn't. To his chagrin, Les Green was signed from Rochdale and proceeded to make 129 consecutive League and Cup appearances.

Goalkeepers really are a special breed. Lonely and isolated, usually only remembered for mistakes, often blamed unfairly, gazing out on freezing cold days from muddy goalmouths, together with a few hundred hardy souls watching reserve-team games. Boulton soldiered on.

Fate then intervened. On Boxing Day 1970, Green had a 'stinker' in a 4-4 draw with Manchester United at the Baseball Ground. Goalkeepers Green and Jimmy Rimmer were both dropped the following week. Les Green never played for Derby County again, but Colin Boulton did. Twenty-two consecutive League and Cup games followed in that season, a championship winners' medal the next – 23 clean sheets – then European Cup glory, highlighted by a wonderful display in a 0-0 draw against Benfica in Lisbon, Eusebio and all, in front of 75,000 in the Stadium of Light. Another championship medal followed and two sets of more than 100 consecutive appearances, as Boulton amassed a total of 334 games, the most ever by a Derby County goalkeeper.

Consistency was undoubtedly the key to Boulton's success. All goalkeepers can make flamboyant saves, but it's the mistakes that count against. Boulton made few mistakes. Even less obvious ones. Not many people remember a Boulton mistake, like they remember Les Green's nightmare, or Gary Sprake of Leeds United. Safe hands were a major asset – he was a good cricketer, too – and his good positional sense made many saves look deceptively easy. He wasn't the tallest, but he dealt with crosses adequately and although not eye-catching in any particular area, his all-round game was so sound. It was honed and perfected in those long days and nights in the reserve team. That prolonged apprenticeship he turned to his subsequent advantage. It was worth the wait.

Jack Bowers – everything a striker should be

JACK Bowers joined Derby County in the same week as Jack Barker. Bowers was 20 years old when he was transferred from Midland League club Scunthorpe United for £150 in May 1928. He went on to become one of the club's best-ever centre-forwards and, after Steve Bloomer, arguably its greatest goalscorer.

When he arrived at Derby, Bowers didn't go straight into the first team. Another great goalscorer, Harry Bedford, occupied the centre-forward berth and Bowers had to wait until February 1929 to make his debut at the Baseball Ground. To accommodate Bowers, manager George Jobey moved Bedford to inside-left against Bolton Wanderers and both players scored in a 2-1 victory. Bowers then hit a hat-trick in the next match, against Portsmouth at Fratton Park, as the Rams recorded a 5-1 victory. The new goalscorer was on his way. Despite that, Bowers was still considered to be too raw for the top flight. He returned down to the Reserves after two more games and Bedford moved back to centre-forward, from where he scored most of his 27 League goals that season. In that first season Bowers played six times and scored five goals as Derby County finished in sixth place in Division One. The following season, 1929-30, Bowers was still waiting. Bedford was an ever-present in 42 League matches and scored 30 goals, as the Rams finished runners-up to Sheffield Wednesday. Bowers played in only three matches, but he did score in each one.

Season 1930-31 established Jack Bowers' reputation, although it didn't start well. Bedford still occupied the centre-forward position, but Jobey was conscious that Bowers's claims could not be ignored. Despite being undefeated for the first eight games of the season, a 2-0 defeat at Portsmouth in the next match prompted Jobey to recall Bowers to lead the attack. He reappeared against Arsenal and scored in a 4-2 victory in front of a crowd of nearly 30,000 at the Baseball Ground. Bowers was back. He never looked back, either. He broke all Derby County's scoring records that season, with 37 goals in 33 League matches. His final tally, in all matches, was 39. The record still stands, although Ray Straw equalled it in 1956-57, in the Third Division North campaign, but in 44 matches. In an amazing spell through January and February, Bowers scored 17 goals in eight matches, four of which were won and four of which were lost. Twenty-five goals for and 26 goals against was the Rams' record over that period. Amazing stuff. The Rams also lost the final three matches of the season, all away, and finished sixth in Division One. Being knocked out of the FA Cup by Exeter City, in front of 16,500 at St James Park, wasn't something that was bargained for. The scoreline was 3-2 and although Bowers scored both goals, it wasn't all glory, glory, even in those days.

Fearless is the word most often used by those who saw him play, diving headers were his speciality: "Jack was a tremendous player. I've seen him dive down here into a load of boots. Jack was two-footed as well," said Tommy Powell. He was tall, excellent in the air and was everything a traditional centre-forward should be and in his 203 League appearances for Derby County he scored 167 goals. He was capped three times for England in 1933-34. Early in the following season he received a severe knee injury when colliding with the railings at the Osmaston End. The injury troubled him the rest of his career and maybe it was one of the reasons he was suddenly sold to Leicester City in November 1936.

After the war, he returned to Derby County as assistant trainer. His role was primarily to be in charge of the reserve team on match days and be in the treatment room, in his white coat, during the week. There, his wry humour and quiet, conscientious manner endeared him to numerous young players. Ron Webster recalls, "Jack Bowers used to come in and say, 'You've just not got that bit of...' I used to like Jack. He used to talk to me and help me. 'You're just lacking that extra skill around the box and whatever, but you're good at defending.' 'In the end,' he said, 'you'll come to full-back.' Then when Cloughie came, he put me there anyway."

Confidence in the skill of the physiotherapist is crucial for any injured player. With Jack Bowers, you always felt you were in safe hands.

Steve Buckley – calm authority

STEVE Buckley is unique among Derby County players. He is the only player in the club's history to register two sets of century appearances, in the League, for Derby County. He made 117 appearances from January 1978 to November 1980 and 122 appearances from November 1983 to May 1986. Only eight other players have ever made a single century of consecutive League appearances. Colin Boulton and Jack Nicholas achieved two sets of century of appearances in all matches. They and Buckley join nine others to have passed that mark.

His first century began on his debut against Nottingham Forest, at the Baseball Ground, in front of a crowd of 33,384. That was in Division One. His second century ended against Darlington, at Feethams, in front of a crowd of 3,585. That was in Division Three. It indicates the difficult times through which Buckley played for Derby County, although the club did gain promotion from Division Three in his final season. Needless to say, he was an ever-present in four of his nine seasons at Derby County, a tribute to his rare consistency.

He was signed by Tommy Docherty from Luton Town for £165,000, but when Derby County were winning a first League championship, under Brian Clough in 1971-72, Buckley was scoring goals for Redfern Athletic in the Midland Sunday League. He originally signed for Ilkeston Town but when he went to Burton Albion, manager Ken Gutteridge converted him from a forward to a left-back. He was transferred to Luton Town as a 20-year-old and spent nearly four seasons at Kenilworth Road, making 123 League appearances for Luton Town. One of those was at the Baseball Ground in May 1975, during Derby County's second championship season, when Roger Davies scored all five goals as Luton were beaten 5-0. Luton were relegated, along with Chelsea and Carlisle United. Teams promoted from Division Two were Norwich City, Aston Villa and Manchester United.

Stocky of build, Buckley had proper footballer's legs. By that I mean he had slightly bandy legs, as though he had just got off a horse. Not many good players have been knock-kneed, although there have been a few notable exceptions. Whatever else, Buckley presented a wide obstacle to get past and not a lot of wingers managed it. As befits someone who started as a left winger, Buckley had good control and like many left-footers, his striking of long passes was easy on the eye. He played with calm authority, rather like Chris Powell, but like Powell, if he got annoyed, sparks could fly. In total he made 366 appearances for Derby County and scored 25 goals, none of which was more spectacular than the first goal in Derby County's 3-2 win against Watford, at the Baseball Ground, in the last match of the 1981-82 season. It was Kevin Hector's final match and Derby County needed a point to be sure of survival in Division Two. A left-foot beauty. Dramatic stuff.

Buckley served under six managers at the Baseball Ground, through troubled times. He also broke a leg against Charlton Athletic in April 1983 and found that Peter Taylor had put him on the transfer list the following season, while he was still recovering. Arthur Cox reinstated him and he went on to be an ever-present in the promotion from Division Three, in 1985-86. He left Derby County at the end of that season, to join Lincoln City. Later, he played for Boston United and eventually became assistant manager of Boston in 1991. He also did some scouting for brother Alan, when he was manager of Grimsby Town and West Bromwich Albion.

Jimmy Bullions – the modest Cup winner

JIMMY Bullions's photograph is on the March 2001 edition of the *County Golfer* magazine for Derbyshire. This is an extract: 'When Derby County went on the Wembley trail, manager Stuart McMillan came out with a simple statement which significantly altered the lifestyle, in later years, of several soccer stars. "If you don't play golf, you'll have to caddie for them that do." In no time at all, Jim had been to Elliott and Crooks (Derbyshire CCC and Rams) at The Spot, Derby to the sports shop to buy his leather bag full of clubs and took up the game he loves today.'

McMillan was a good enough golfer to represent Derbyshire and in 1949, Johnny Morris made part of his transfer to Derby County from Manchester United conditional on being able to join Kedleston Park Golf Club. For many clubs Wednesday was golf day although Don Revie, a keen golfer himself, banned Leeds United players from playing after Wednesday because it was, in his words, 'a strolling game' and he didn't want 'strolling' players on a Saturday. 'Bonding' is the current word for such collective get-togethers, although La Manga, rather than the local golf club, seems to suit modern fashion.

The article continues: 'Jim recalls that right winger Sammy Crooks (who was forced by injury to miss the Final – hence Reg Harrison's inclusion) was the best golfer of the bunch. The team's Trent bus driver was encouraged to have a day off to visit London while the team were in Luton. This enabled Sammy to drive the bus, with team aboard, to play a round at Harpenden Golf Club. Don't even bother to ask what the insurance consequences of that little escapade would be by today's standards, with such a precious cargo of stars involved.'

Jimmy Bullions is now 76 years old and, with Reg Harrison, the only survivor of that FA Cup-winning team. In 1946 he was 22, the youngest on the pitch at Wembley, and he remembers incidents in the match with great clarity: "I was behind Jack Stamps, right behind him, and he volleyed this ball and from where I was it looked a goal all the way. I thought: 'By, this is going in.' Jack loved to volley them, you know. They'd go over the top and all over, but he loved to volley the ball. Anyway, he really hit this one and then, on its path, it went... phut. Do you know, I've never seen any film, or anything, pictures, whatever, of the ball actually bursting."

Bullions went down the pit at 15 years old and played for Chesterfield as an amateur. He joined Derby County in 1944 and played regularly in the two years before the end of the war, a total of 74 appearances. He slightly resents the fact that his appearances for Derby County are listed as 17, because only peacetime football is used for record purpose, but he played in all the FA Cup rounds in 1945-46 and his position was never threatened in that run. After the war Tim Ward, back from military service, regained the number-four shirt and Bullions moved to Leeds United in 1947, where he played 34 League matches. In 1950 he joined Sammy Crooks at Shrewsbury Town and made 131 League appearances as Shrewsbury became established as a Football League club. Jack Stamps and Rams full-back Jack Parr also joined Crooks at Gay Meadow. Bullions later played locally for Worksop Town, Gresley Rovers, Matlock Town and then as player-manager and manager of Alfreton Town.

He's typically modest about his style of play: "I loved playing at the Baseball Ground. It slowed all the others down to my speed! It's not surprising players got the ball stuck under their feet in such conditions and with someone like me ploughing into them, they often packed it in." These days, courtesy of Lionel Pickering, who values the contribution of former players greatly, he has a seat in the directors' box at Pride Park. He sits with Angus Morrison, who also played in the Cup run in 1946, together with his long-time friend and colleague, Reg Harrison. Three times a week, Jimmy Bullions plays golf.

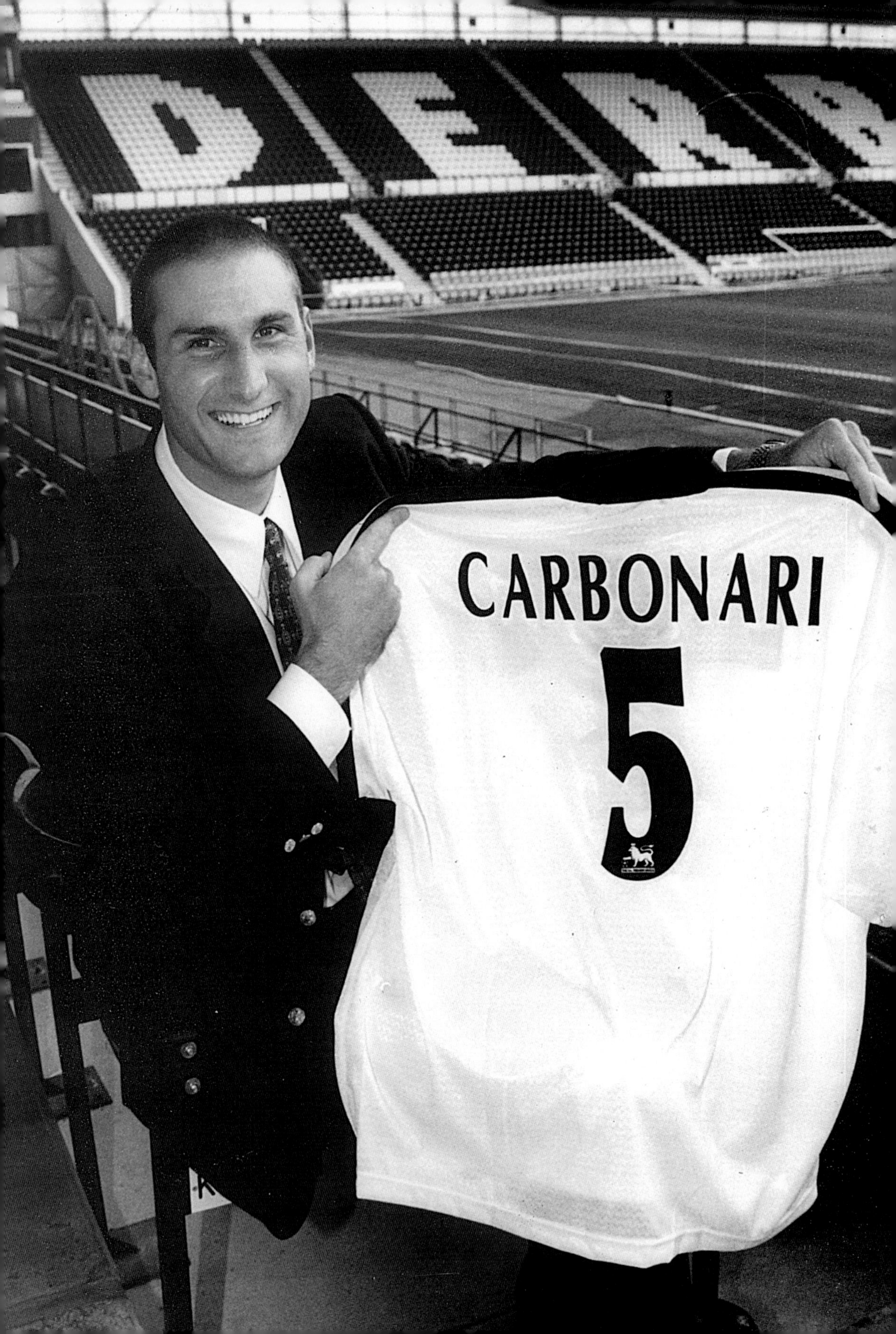
CARBONARI
5

Horacio Carbonari – good feet for a big lad

HORACIO Carbonari was Derby County's record transfer fee when he joined the club. He cost £2.8 million when he was signed from Rosario Central, in Argentina, in May 1998. One of the attractions for Derby County was that Carbonari holds an Italian passport and so comes under the regulations for European Union players. Clubs are only allowed to play three non-European nationals at any one time.

There have been some great centre-halves in Derby County's history. Archie Goodall, Jack Barker, Leon Leuty, Roy McFarland, Mark Wright and Igor Stimac would have graced any team in any era. Carbonari has a difficult task to break into that bracket, but he is on the way. Sometimes criticised for lack of pace – even Bobby Moore had that cross to bear – Carbonari usually makes up for that with really good football skills and his work at close quarters is outstanding. Not many spectators appreciate what happens in crowded penalty areas, it's easier to see happenings in open play, but Carbonari reads situations well, watches the ball closely and in one-against-one situations, especially near the goal-line, is seldom beaten. His concentration, too, is improving and the mistakes which marred consistency levels in his early Derby County days are now less prevalent. Archie Gemmill's assessment that Carbonari would be an outstanding player is looking valid.

What do others think? Steve Powell: "I think he's an excellent player. I think he's got the potential to be in the top bracket, but it's difficult to say. He may need to move on to a bigger club to do that. I don't know whether he can achieve that at Derby." Geoff Hazledine: "He's a mystery to me. Sometimes he looks a class act and then, he looks really leaden-footed... but he does some wonderful things. He's got great composure. As we all know, he strikes a ball well, and then, at other times, the contrast is so great that you cannot believe it's the same person in the same shirt. He seems to get lost in the game, sometimes." Graham Richards: "I think he's an outstanding player, whose reading of the game is excellent and whose contribution going forward will be one of the aspects of his game that will improve. He scored more goals in his last year in Argentina than some acknowledged out-and-out strikers did. That shows two things, one of which is that Carbonari is a good footballer." Phil Waller: "He's got good feet for a big lad, hasn't he? It's a big step when they come from the continent, or even further. It was a big enough step for us when we moved ten miles down the road!"

In possession, Carbonari is impressive. When most defenders find themselves in opposing penalty areas, they still play like defenders. They look out of place. Carbonari doesn't. When in forward positions, he plays like a forward and his close control and awareness means he can create chances for others, although the first thing – and sometimes last thing – on his mind, is to create a chance for himself. As befits a man who earned the nickname 'Petaco' ('Bazooka') in Argentina, Carbonari likes a shot at goal. That sometimes leads to fairly heated discussions with all and sundry, when a free-kick presents itself anything up to 40 yards out. So far, his reputation outweighs his productivity with such opportunities.

What isn't in doubt are the sweeping passes out to the right wing, hit with the outside of the right foot, which, for older supporters, brings to mind images of the great Jack Barker in his prime. Roy Christian: "He [Barker] was a good footballer as well, but what I remember were those lovely pass out to the wings that he gave. Like Carbonari, who is good at that, too. He [Barker] had good ball control. Centre halves weren't always good footballers, but he was..." 'Petaco' Carbonari has much to live up to.

Willie Carlin – marvellous wee footballer

WILLIE Carlin came from Liverpool and was born in 1940, which made him a 'war baby'. He signed as a professional for Liverpool Football Club in 1958, which was around the same time as Bill Shankly became manager. Carlin always says he was privileged to be at Anfield at a time when the legendary 'Shanks' was laying the foundations which made Liverpool the most powerful force in English football. Those early experiences never left Carlin. He was and still is football daft, as they say, especially on Merseyside. When you listen to him banging on about something or other that happened in the second half of a match a week last Tuesday, you know for a fact that what Carlin really means is that, if only he could get his boots on right then, he'd show people what 'so and so' should really have done. To say Willie Carlin was a combative footballer is like saying Don Bradman could play cricket. Despite a great affinity for Derby, Carlin's spiritual home is Liverpool and, if you've got the time, he'll give you chapter and verse about 'Shanks'. Carlin played for the England Youth team but made only one appearance in the first team at Anfield. By the time he joined Derby County, he'd been a professional for ten years. Much of that time had been spent in the lower leagues, with Halifax Town, Carlisle United and Sheffield United. Rugby League is the bigger sport in Halifax and when he told people he played soccer for Town, he says they looked sorry for him.

During their period at Hartlepools, Brian Clough and Peter Taylor were made well aware of the little midfield general, who could bite a bit if required and wasn't slow at organising people around him.

The move to the Baseball Ground surprised him. He was settled in Sheffield, but Clough was in one of his 'brooking no argument moods', even from Carlin, so he signed for £60,000, which was a Rams record fee at the time. When he got to Derby, Clough simply told him, "Go out and play." As Carlin explains, "What really happened was that Dave Mackay took the back four and I, sort of, took midfield and up front." Clough and Taylor knew their man. The Rams embarked on a run of 13 matches undefeated and by the end of the season were Second Division champions.

At 5ft 4ins tall, Carlin was a skilful all-round midfielder, who could control the pace of a game with his neat passing and shrewd football brain. He'd broken his leg at Carlisle, which may partly have accounted for a rather jerky running style, but there was no doubting his commitment and he could be a fierce tackler. Like Archie Gemmill, who replaced him as Derby County's midfield dynamo, he irritated opponents. He especially irritated them when he ran the ball to the corners of the pitch, in the dying minutes of a game, in order to protect a lead, or a point. When Carlin got wedged alongside the corner flag, with two or three opponents snapping and scrapping around him like dogs fighting over a bone, he was in his element. It was then the crowd really appreciated Carlin's Liverpool upbringing.

Then, quite suddenly, he was gone. If the move to Derby County surprised him, the transfer to Leicester City surprised him even more. It also saddened him. He reasoned he was still playing well and didn't want to go. He did have arthritis, though – most players did – and he believes it was the reason why Clough and Taylor let him go. He wasn't finished however. He won another promotion, from Division Two with Leicester City, and a further promotion, with Notts County, from Division Three. He finished his career at Cardiff City, having made 423 League appearances, scoring 74 goals. "Tough little guy and a marvellous wee footballer," said Dave Mackay and you can't get better testament than that.

Raich Carter – immense self belief

RAICH Carter was one of the most charismatic figures ever to play for Derby County. Indeed, he was one of the most charismatic figures ever to play football. Silver hair, stocky build and immense self-belief, Carter oozed authority. He would certainly have had a huge impact in any era.

"I never saw Raich under pressure," said double-international Willie Watson, who played with Carter at Sunderland. "He carried empty space around with like an umbrella."

Like all great players he knew his own worth. Some thought him arrogant – he once said that Sunderland were stupid to sell him for only £6,000 and Derby were lucky to get him for that – but for most who played with him and others who knew him later, he had a dry sense of humour and was fun to be with. Did he believe himself to have been the best footballer who ever lived? Quite possibly and, at various points during his illustrious career, there were more than a few who were prepared to agree with him. What is without doubt is that together with Steve Bloomer and Hughie Gallacher, Raich Carter was one of Derby County's all-time 'greats' of British football.

I saw him play once. He was with Hull City at the time and I was about eight or nine years old, on holiday in Scarborough. As a special treat my father took me on a yellow and black East Yorkshire Traction double- decker bus, along the coast road to see Carter play an early-season match at Hull. Of course, I can't remember anything about the game, but in my mind's eye there is a vague impression of a rather portly figure directing operations from the centre-circle, much like the conductor of a symphony orchestra. I'm told he also used to take all the corners, free-kicks and penalties – it was said that he 'refereed' a few matches as well – but he also made time to score 53 goals in 136 appearances for Hull City, to go with the 34 goals he scored in only 63 appearances for Derby County. (Remember he also played as a 'guest' for Derby County during wartime.) In 1949, as player-manager, he guided Hull City to promotion from the Third Division North with average attendances of more than 37,000 at Boothferry Park, most of whom had come, like us, to see him. He was still a hero in that city when he died there in 1996.

In 1962 Tim Ward succeeded Harry Storer as manager of Derby County. His first move in September of that year was to transfer me to Mansfield Town. The manager at Field Mill was Raich Carter. Despite being in his 50s, he still liked the occasional outing in five-a-sides; always demanding the ball, shielding it, guiding it, cajoling it and everybody else around, as we all tried, unsuccessfully, to catch him in possession. It was quite obvious that he was something special. He didn't come into the dressing- room much, just now and again, when he fancied an argument. He liked an argument did Raich and in a dressing-room which contained a few strong personalities, it wasn't long before the fur was flying. "Puskas? Puskas? Give me Peter Doherty," he'd say and away they'd go, about how he was behind the times and the game was different now. He'd have a jolly alright, but he could always pull in the reins when necessary and everybody knew where the mark was and not to step over it.

He left at Christmas, to go to Middlesbrough. The young players he developed at Mansfield, like Mike Stringfellow at Leicester, Peter Morris at Ipswich and Norwich and Ken Wagstaff at Hull City, went on to bigger things, but they were all there at his funeral, eventually. The first thing that went when he left was the full-length oil painting, which hung behind his desk in the manager's office, of himself in his England kit, with his foot on the old leather ball. He knew his own value, did Raich.

Two years later, the Mansfield team were having lunch in the Queen's Hotel in Manchester, prior to a match in Lancashire. Middlesbrough had already dined in a different part of the hotel and their team coach, complete with police outriders, was ready to depart. Suddenly, the door opened and in came Raich. The only two players left at Mansfield from the team he'd managed were Peter Morris and myself and, really, he'd no reason to waste his time on us. As traffic piled up in Piccadilly and the local constabulary became more and more agitated, Raich had a chat with us.

How were we getting on? Were we enjoying playing? Make sure we always played with confidence. The world could have stood still and, for a short while, it did. That was the thing about Raich Carter, he made you feel a million dollars. Sheer class.

Brian Clough – he took the breath away

THERE is very little that hasn't been said about Brian Clough, either by other people, or by Clough himself. Clough, on directors: "There's a seven-man board at Derby and I wouldn't give tuppence for five of them." On players: "It doesn't matter if the players like you or dislike you. It's when they respect you that they play for you." On football intelligence: "Show me a talented player who is thick and I'll show you a player who has problems." On Yorkshire County Cricket Club's sacking of Geoffrey Boycott in 1986: "I don't know of any other club in history which finished bottom of the league, sacked its star player and left the manager in the job. The Yorkshire Committee are guilty of the biggest whitewash I can recall."

Being a Yorkshireman, born in Middlesbrough in 1935, Clough would have a view on such matters. Besides which, he liked cricket and Boycott was a kindred spirit. On the imminent signing of Nigel Jemson in 1988: "I haven't seen the lad, but my coaches have and he also comes hugely recommended by my greengrocer." Perhaps there lies a clue to Clough's enduring popularity with the public. Despite the tongue-in-cheek quotation, he never lost sight of the fact that football is 'The People's Game'. More than anything, Clough identified with people.

Hunter Davies, in *The Kingswood Book Of Football*, writes: 'There were shouts of delight as he arrived home in his Mercedes. He was slightly late for the party, but they were all waiting for him, 16 eight-year-old boys. The party was for Simon, his eldest. He has another son, Nigel, six and a daughter Elizabeth, who is five. He went in, clapped his hands and told them to get ready. He has had 14 kids in his Mercedes, but he decided 16 was too many, so they all set off down the suburban street, running behind him, shouting, "We are the Champions." We got to the park and he arranged two sides and started them playing. He was to be the referee, although Elizabeth was to stay beside him and do the actual whistle-blowing.

'An onlooker could easily have thought he was slightly deranged. He wasn't running a children's party game between two sets of eight-year-olds. It was deadly serious. He treated the kids as real professional footballers, which of course they responded to. He padded up and down in his carpet slippers, screaming out instructions, like the schoolmaster in the football match in *Kes* who was convinced he was running Manchester United.

'"Do that once more, Si, and you're off!" he shouted at his eight-year-old son. "Who said you could pick that ball up? The whistle didn't blow for a throw-in, did it? No, it did not. Handball!"

'He let them get away with nothing, not even foul throw-ins, though their little arms weren't really up to it. He made them line up while he demonstrated the correct way.

'Even his five-year-old daughter Elizabeth, who was supposed to blow every time he told her, didn't escape his wrath. "I've warned you, Lib. If you bugger around any more, I'll take the whistle."

'His wife Barbara was duly grateful when they all trailed back to the house for the birthday tea, all nicely quietened and exhausted. He watched them getting stuck into the goodies then went into his front room and opened a bottle of champagne.'

From the day Brian Clough arrived at the Baseball Ground in 1967, to the day he left in 1973, he lit up the town. Suddenly things were happening to Derby County. A brilliantly-executed promotion from the Second Division, where the club had been becalmed for years, exhilarating victories over some of the best teams in the land, a first-ever League championship for the club, and pulsating nights of European Cup football. It took the breath away. No wonder he is the only man who could also manage Nottingham Forest to glory and they'd still put up a statue to him in Derby.

You take people as you find them: "Conceited, arrogant, er...generous." These are his words, not mine.

For my part, I've always found Brian Clough considerate and helpful on occasions when I've asked for assistance about something or other, which was important to me but inconsequential to him. His contribution to Derby County was immense and the enjoyment that thousands of supporters experienced when they watched his teams play is what football is supposed to be about.

Most of all in my mind's eye I think not of Clough the manager, but of Clough the player. Beautifully balanced, 12 yards out, short backswing, usually right foot, sometimes on the half-turn, clinical low shot... GOAL! There's no substitute for playing, even in the park. Brian Clough will tell you that. So you'd better believe it

George Collin – he stopped the others

KIRBY; Cooper, Collin; Nicholas, Barker, Keen. The names used to roll off supporters' tongues in the early 1930s as surely as night follows day. Once Jack Kirby replaced Harry Wilkes in goal around Christmas 1932, the back six of Derby County's team sheet could have been set in stone. Of those six, George Collin was probably the least celebrated.

Collin was signed by George Jobey in November 1927 from North-Eastern League side West Stanley, where he had returned after breaking his leg whilst playing for Bournemouth. Eighteen months earlier, Jobey had signed right-back Tommy Cooper from Port Vale and the pair went on to record a total of 600 appearances between them, 207 being in partnership with each other. They had another thing in common, too. Neither was a goalscorer. Cooper's solitary goal in a 5-2 defeat of Middlesbrough in February 1932 was the only goal either of them scored in their careers. At least that goal was at the Baseball Ground, so at least some supporters could say: "I was there." It must be remembered, of course, that until Arsenal introduced the 'third back', or 'stopper' centre-half in the early 1930s, as a consequence of the change in the offside law in 1925, the centre-half was expected to attack as well as defend. Rather like in netball, he was the fulcrum of the team. Jack Barker was Derby County's last attacking centre-half and even he had alter the style he grew up with, as the new formation began to take effect. In the old system, someone had to stay back and defend full-time, which was the role of the full-backs and to which Collin was ideally suited.

Ironically, it was an injury to Cooper that allowed Collin to make his debut, in a 4-4 draw against Cardiff City at Ninian Park. Billy Carr switched from left-back to right to allow Collin to make his debut and The *Derby Evening Telegraph* reported: 'Collin's play indicates that Mr Jobey has found in him a class young back. This nicely made defender was very cool, and in manoeuvre and kicking was very discriminate.' Collin was an ever-present in season 1932-33 and in one sequence missed only four games out of a possible 136. He occupies 20th place in the Derby County list of appearances in all matches, with 334, and is 18th in the League matches list with 309.

Tall and quite lean, he was not a delicate type of player. Harry Storer used to say, "There are only two types of players in football. Those who can play and those than can stop the others." Collins belonged to the latter category and was noted for his strong tackling. He was also a good kicker of the ball and as local historian and broadcaster, Roy Christian, observes, "He believed that if something was there to be kicked, he would kick it – first time – if possible." He was one of only three Derby County players to be sent off, at Sunderland, in the whole of the period between the two World Wars. The others were Bill Paterson and Bert Fairclough, who were both centre-forwards. Coincidentally, Collin left Derby County to join Sunderland in the close season of 1936 after Jobey signed Jack Howe. He later played with Port Vale and Burton Town, and retired to live in Derby. He died in February 1989.

More a Michael Forsyth than a Geoff Barrowcliffe in style and appearance, Collin was, for Cooper, the perfect partner

Tommy Cooper – polished and poised

FISH and chips, Laurel and Hardy, Morecambe and Wise, peaches and cream go together just like Tommy Cooper and George Collin, who were Derby County's full-backs for much of the time that George Jobey was manager of the club. Like the examples given, they were very much opposites as players, but many older supporters would no doubt agree with Roy Christian, who claims that they were 'the best I've ever seen as a combination'.

Collin was taller, standing over six feet in height, more angular in build, more ponderous in movement, but was less skilful in his distribution and lacked the class that came more naturally to his snowy-haired partner. For Cooper was one of the best full-backs ever to wear the Derby County shirt and he also captained England. He played 15 times for England between 1927 and 1935 and was also picked for the Football League on five occasions.

Unfortunately, the World Cup passed him by. It was staged for the first time in 1930 and the hosts, Uruguay won it, but the four home nations ignored it, ostensibly because of a row over payments to amateurs. Certainly Tommy Cooper would have graced the competition and there is little doubt that he would have played more for England had he not suffered cartilage trouble which necessitated the removal of damaged cartilages from both knees. In those days such an operation was very serious and the recovery rate, at least completely, was not impressive.

Cooper was a native of the Potteries and played for Trentham in the Cheshire League before joining Port Vale. He made 266 appearances for Derby County and to say that his transfer from Port Vale, for £2,500 in 1926, proved to be a bargain would be an understatement. 'Polished' is the word which is most often used to describe his play. Bert Mozley and Geoff Barrowcliffe, rather than Tony Conwell and Martin McDonnell. In an era when full-backs were first and foremost defenders, he brought a touch of style to the position which was not often seen. Says Ernie Hallam, who has seen them all in a lifetime of supporting the Rams, "He was, perhaps, my all-time favourite."

Cooper captained Derby County from November 1931, when he took over from Johnny McIntyre, until he was transferred to Liverpool for £8,000 in December 1934. At Anfield, he was immediately made captain and joined up with his partner in the England team, former Sheffield Wednesday left-back Ernest Blenkinsop. He played for Liverpool up to the outbreak of war, making around 160 appearances for the Anfield club, but his career came to a tragic end. He joined the Military Police when war broke out and while serving as a sergeant, aged 36, he was killed in a road accident in June 1940, when the motor cycle he was riding collided with a double-decker bus. He was buried in Nottingham Road cemetery in Derby. His son, also Tommy and who bears a striking resemblence to his father, was for many years a well-known referee in local Derbyshire football.

Arthur Cox – individually and collectively

ARTHUR Cox was appointed manager of Derby County at one of the lowest points in the history of the club. His contribution to the club's revival cannot be overstated, although the later years were clouded with disappointment as Lionel Pickering's money failed to bring the anticipated success and Cox's big-money signings flattered to deceive.

At the end of the 1983-84 season, Derby County's situation was dire. Bankruptcy in the High Court just averted, thanks to a last-ditch rescue operation mounted by Stuart Webb, relegation could not be escaped. It was in such unpromising circumstances that Arthur Cox took charge.

Cox was unusual as a manager in that he had never been a player, not unless his junior days at Coventry City are counted. As an 18-year-old, he broke his leg and turned to coaching. He coached the youth team at Coventry for four years and was then chief coach at Walsall and Aston Villa, under Tommy Docherty. He moved as coach to Preston North End in 1970, then to Halifax Town as assistant manager and to Blackpool in the same capacity. He was assistant to Bob Stokoe when Sunderland beat Leeds United 1-0 in the 1973 FA Cup Final. In 1976 he was coaching Galatasaray in Turkey before in October of that year he obtained his first manager's job, at Chesterfield. In 1979-80, Chesterfield missed promotion to Division Two by one point, but Cox spent quite heavily by Chesterfield's standards and when he left for Newcastle United, in September 1980, Spireites supporters blamed him for the club's debts.

Cox had success at Newcastle. He signed Kevin Keegan, Chris Waddle from Tow Law Town, Peter Beardsley from Vancouver Whitecaps and Terry McDermott from Liverpool. Exciting times returned to St James's Park and Newcastle were promoted from Division Two in 1984. A fortnight later, Cox resigned 'on a matter of principle' and Webb persuaded him to join Derby County.

Most of Cox's early signings at Derby were successful. Rob Hindmarch, Eric Steele, Gary Micklewhite, Geraint Williams, Trevor Christie, Ross Maclaren, Jeff Chandler, John Gregory, Mel Sage, Michael Forsyth, Phil Gee, Nigel Callaghan and others, all had parts to play as Derby County swept from the Third to the First Division in successive seasons and Cox could do no wrong. With Derby County in Division One, Robert Maxwell began to take an interest. Peter Shilton, Mark Wright and Dean Saunders arrived, as did Ted McMinn, and the Rams finished fifth in 1988-89. Then it started to go wrong. Derby County finished 16th in 1989-90 and in September, Maxwell announced that the club was up for sale. The effect was catastrophic as the Rams plunged to relegation.

Enter Lionel Pickering and an era of false promise as Cox signed £1 million players left, right and centre. Even one of the club's unofficial fanzines was entitled *Hey, Big Spender*. Expectations rose, but despite reaching the play-offs against Blackburn Rovers, promotion was denied and disillusionment set in. Pickering decided enough was enough and took over as chairman from Brian Fearn, after an acrimonious EGM. In October 1993, Cox left Derby, suffering from a bad back.

Cox was at Derby County for nine years, the club's longest-serving manager after George Jobey and it's unfortunate that his early achievements were soured by later events. As at Chesterfield, Cox showed he was not as good a manager with money, as he was without it. Maybe he was really a coach at heart. His later career saw him follow Kevin Keegan to Fulham and then England in that capacity.

Few players speak anything other than highly of Cox, despite his gravelly voice, reputation for being a disciplinarian and taciturn manner. Eric Steele says, "He had this image of a sergeant-major. I thought he was very fair. I respected him greatly for the three years I played here because he would tell you straight. He'd tell you on a Tuesday if you weren't playing. He wouldn't hang about. Some managers wait. At least you knew where you stood and I think the players respected that."

Steve Sutton says, "I think if he made a mistake it was in bringing too many kids too soon into the side. I think the core of experience went and with that went a little bit of discipline because the kids didn't respect him. They didn't respect him as I respected him and as the players who had been here respected him. I think that caused him a few problems and it didn't work out with the kids, as we all know to our cost." As Cox might say, in that distinctive West Midlands accent: "Individually and collectively..." Then again, he might not.

Sammy Crooks – just a lovely bloke

OUTSIDE-RIGHT Sammy Crooks played for England 26 times. He actually played more times for England between the two World Wars than Stanley Matthews and he was undoubtedly one of Derby County's best-loved figures. His association with the club spanned 40 years and, with the town of Derby, it was for most of his life, although he was born in County Durham and was signed by George Jobey from Durham City, for £300, in 1927. For Derby he played in 445 matches and scored 111 goals after 'stepping off a coal lorry on Thursday'.

"Sammy was so direct in everything he did. He was a straight-forward winger really, but he got a move on," said George Collin, who played full- back in the 1930s. Crooks missed the 1946 Cup Final because of injury. The decision was marginal and Sammy must have been extremely disappointed, but it made for a fairytale opportunity for his young deputy, Reg Harrison, who always acknowledges the help and encouragement he received from Crooks. For those who knew him, they would expect no less. In Tommy Powell's phrase, "He was a lovely bloke."

Crooks served two spells as chief scout with Derby County. The first began in 1946, when he was still a player, and ended in 1949. He returned as chief scout in 1960, having filled various roles at clubs like Retford Town, Shrewsbury Town, Gresley Rovers, Burton Albion and Heanor Town. He could spot a player. It was on his advice that Tim Ward signed Kevin Hector. "He was just like a good golfer. When he hit the ball it just went where he was aiming," said Crooks about Hector, reflecting his other great passion, golf.

Sammy Crooks's enthusiasm for football was infectious. Of course, I never saw him play, but I did play with him. In 1960, he succeeded Charlie Elliott as chief scout, and on Tuesday mornings I used to attend Derby Technical College on Normanton Road. I then had to train in the afternoon. After the running part, trainer Ralph Hann would send me to the 'shooting box', which was situated under the Main Stand where the press office was eventually sited. As I banged the ball around in the box, the noise would carry along the corridors to Sammy's office. After a while, I'd hear him coming. You could always hear him coming. He had little metal 'segs' in the toes and heels of his shoes, to protect them from wearing out. On the concrete floors of the passages, his footsteps echoed, clickety-click, clickety-click. It sounded more like Sammy Davis Jnr than a club official.

When he arrived, he could never keep still. "Try this, what about that," he'd say, hopping about like a child in the playground and, every so often, having a go himself, even with his 'segs' on. We had a few little competitions and he was always reluctant to leave when someone came to tell him the telephone hadn't stopped ringing. I'm told he was a wonderful player. Of course, that must be true, but the person I remember – and played with – was simply, just such 'a lovely bloke'. When he died at Belper in February 1981, he hadn't an enemy in the world.

Bill Curry – he loved scoring goals

BILL Curry was a rumbustious centre-forward, brought to Derby County by manager Harry Storer in the close season of 1959. He was signed from Brighton and Hove Albion for a fee of £12,000, which was quite a lot more than the Rams had paid for a player for some considerable time. A former England under-23 international, Curry scored for Newcastle United in the first-ever League match played under floodlights, at Fratton Park, Portsmouth, on 22 February 1956. At the Baseball Ground he quickly became a crowd favourite with his all-action style and useful scoring record. He played 148 League matches and scored 67 goals in the old Division Two, which puts him 17th in the Rams all-time list and in all matches for Derby County he scored 76 goals in 164 appearances.

Curry was very much an old-fashioned centre-forward. Not tall and favouring his left foot strongly, he led the forward line in traditional style, often having real ding-dong battles with raw-boned centre halves, particularly in home matches. Away from home, he could sometimes be more eye-catching than effective. Like Fred Trueman on the cricket field, he had the knack of always giving the impression of maximum effort. Sometimes, though, when a cold December wind was whipping across an icy pitch, you sometimes wished he'd make himself a little more available when some large, nasty opponent was rapidly closing you down in your own half of the field. What you really didn't need was the manager being fooled as well. Storer didn't believe much in team talks, but he once gave a well-remembered one following a dismal defeat at Roker Park, where centre-half Charlie Hurley, recently voted Sunderland's 'Player of the 20th century', hardly broke sweat. Storer's theme was that the only player who should keep his wages that week was Bill Curry. There was much shuffling of feet and looking at the floor when we heard that, I can tell you.

On his day, however, Curry could be a handful, for anyone. Not more than 5ft 10ins in height, he was a real threat in the air, thanks to agility and good timing and he specialised in arriving late for headers, often to the surprise of big defenders. He had reasonable control and was a good target man for balls out of defence and although not the quickest, he had enough strength and determination to hold off defenders when in sight of goal. Most of all, he loved scoring goals and, although he didn't indulge in histrionics, his delight when he did score was palpable. When he put his mind to it, Curry was good to play with.

"What do you think of Bill Curry?" was a casual enquiry by Tommy Cummings, manager of Mansfield Town, one morning before training in January 1965. In November 1964, Ken Wagstaff had been sold to Hull City for £40,000 and the Stags needed a replacement. My reply was that I thought Curry would do a good job, so it wasn't a total surprise when Bill joined Mansfield in February 1965. He had a hard act to follow. Given his chance by Raich Carter, as a 17-year-old, Wagstaff was a local-born hero at Field Mill. No-one needed to worry. As at Derby, Curry became a firm favourite with the fans and scored 57 goals in 113 appearances for the Stags. He settled in the area, but died in August 1990, aged 54. In his career, Bill Curry played 394 League games and scored 178 goals. You can be sure that each one would have given him equal pleasure.

Peter Daniel – the quiet man

IN a crowded room, Peter Daniel is man who doesn't stand out. Not for him the flamboyant gesture, the extrovert personality, the loud voice. Daniel is one of life's quiet men. He is none the worse for that and his Derby County career includes a Division Two promotion under Brian Clough and a League championship winners' medal under Dave Mackay. He was Rams 'Player of the Year' in the club's second championship campaign in 1974-75, when he memorably stood in for the injured Roy McFarland. In his Derby County career he was never really considered a first-team 'regular', but he made 237 appearances, plus nine as a substitute. Not a bad record for the quiet man from Ripley.

It also speaks volumes for Daniel that he was one of the players who survived the Clough 'new broom' in 1967. Not many did. Daniel, in fact, went on to outlast Clough himself at Derby County. In total he played for Derby County at professional level for 15 years, after being signed by Tim Ward as an apprentice in 1963. Others in that group of young players that developed under Ward were Ron Webster, John Richardson, Mick Hopkinson, Phil Waller and Bobby Saxton, whilst Alan Durban and Colin Boulton were Ward signings, who went on to greater glories under Clough and Mackay.

For a while, Daniel played mostly at left-back, despite being a centre-half by inclination. He made his debut, aged 18, against Bristol City at the Baseball Ground in October 1965. A fortnight later he played in the last match that Jack Parry played for Derby County and, remember, Parry signed professional for Derby County in 1948! Daniel didn't miss a match for the rest of that season as Derby County finished eighth in the old Division Two. He continued to play in both full-back positions, making 56 appearances on the left and 32 on the right, before he finally played at centre-half, in October 1969, which was four years after his debut. He came in for the injured McFarland against Manchester City at the Baseball Ground. The attendance was 40,788 and the Rams lost 1-0. That 1969-70 season saw the highest-ever 'gate' at the Baseball Ground, 41,826 against Tottenham Hotspur. It also was the highest average for any season, 35,924, as Derby County finished fourth in Division One. In that first season back in Division One, Clough used a total of only 17 players, of which five, including Daniel (eight), made only 17 appearances between them.

Daniel continued to make occasional appearances in the next two years, but he didn't play at all in the 1971-72 championship season, when Clough used a total of 16 players and three of those made a total of six appearances between them. Good teamwork was one of the key ingredients in the Clough era and you don't get that by change. Daniel did, however, play a big part in the Reserves' success in winning the Central League title in the same season.

His big chance came in 1974-75. McFarland ruptured an Achilles tendon playing for England at Wembley and Dave Mackay sent for Daniel. He says, "Was I tempted to buy when McFarland was injured? No. Peter Daniel had always done well. Yes, Peter Daniel and Colin Todd did well. Colin Todd was the PFA Player of the Year, because he was doing what McFarland was doing previously, as a leader. He was a bigger man, not in size, but in status than Peter Daniel, but he was a super guy, Pete Daniel." That could be the finest compliment of all, for the quiet man.

Glyn Davies – up and at 'em

GLYN Davies was a sharp-tackling defender who took over as captain of Derby County from Reg Ryan. It was quite a contrast. Ryan, an Irishman, was a thoughtful, scheming inside-forward with a polished style, whereas Davies, a Welshman, was an 'up and at 'em' type of player whose enthusiasm and abrasiveness tended to disguise many technical deficiencies. As far as supporters and management were concerned, opinion was often split as to Glyn Davies's contributions. As far as Davies was concerned, there was no disagreement. Football began with effort, more effort and most effort and, as captain, he led from the front. Davies had little time for frills and marks for artistic merit. His marks were usually on the shins and ankles of opposition forwards and he fitted well into Harry Storer's Derby County defence of the late 1950s and early 1960s.

That defence took few prisoners. Les Moore, Frank Upton, Tony Conwell and Davies, backed by either Ken Oxford or Reg Matthews, were not to be taken lightly and many an opposing forward had the bruises to prove it. Unfortunately, although opponents often suffered, the goals against column suffered also. A good example was in season 1960-61, when Derby County scored 80 goals. Unfortunately, they also conceded 80 goals, which left the club in 12th place in the old Second Division as Alf Ramsey's Ipswich Town were promoted as champions ahead of runners-up Sheffield United. Liverpool finished third, Middlesbrough fifth, Sunderland sixth and Leeds United were behind the Rams, in 14th place.

Davies had signed professional forms for Derby County as long ago as 1949, but it was four years before his debut. He played exactly 200 League matches for the Rams before returning to his home town, Swansea, in 1962. He then had a spell as player-manager of Yeovil Town, before returning to Swansea, as manager in June 1965. During his 15 months as manager of Swansea Town, he encountered Giorgio Chinaglia.

'The Giorgio Chinaglia Story' is the sub-title of a recent book, *Arrivederci Swansea*, by Mario Risoli, which chronicles the amazing tale of a player who was rejected and released by Swansea Town in 1966. He then went on to play for Lazio, became an Italian international, went to America to play with Pele and Franz Beckenbauer at New York Cosmos, in 1999 was inducted into the US Soccer Hall of Fame, was voted Lazio's Player of the Century, became president of the Cosmos, returned home to Italy and bought Lazio. The manager who released him from Swansea Town was – Glyn Davies!

It is fair to say that whilst he was at Swansea, Chinaglia was difficult to handle. He was brought up in Cardiff where his father Mario had a restaurant. Giorgio joined Swansea as an apprentice and went off the rails, having more money than most young players at that time, with a penchant for fast women, slow horses and cards. Said Davies, "I'd got fed up with Giorgio as a person, because he'd become a nuisance. Whatever we tried to do didn't work... His general attitude was wrong. It's no good quarrelling and having upsets, and Giorgio developed this attitude. We were worried about his behaviour rubbing off. It's easier to follow a bad egg than a good one. In some respects I wasn't happy to see him go because he had quality, but in other respects I was glad, because he had become a disruptive influence. There was no way he was going to stay at Swansea."

Some Swansea players took a different view. Said Keith Todd, "As a manger you've got to know every individual and treat them differently. I don't think Glyn was very good at that. He wielded the stick and that doesn't always work. Giorgio was at Swansea at the wrong time and with the wrong manager." David Ward said, "He should have had a lot more counselling and direction. They were hitting him in his pocket rather than getting him in a room and trying to sort the problem out." Alan Jones: "You'll never get the best out of people if you have a go at them in front of others."

Chinaglia was given a free transfer. He moved to Massese in Italy's Serie C. Three years later he was one of the hottest properties in Italian football and was transferred to Lazio for £140,000, which was a massive fee in those days. "I always thought he had a chance," said Glyn Davies. "What he achieved at Lazio didn't surprise me." What Chinaglia said about Swansea was appreciative: "The best thing they ever did was give me a free transfer. It changed my life. I will always thank Swansea for that." And Glyn Davies?

Roger Davies – awkward to play against

ROGER Davies has never lost his enthusiasm for playing football. He's in his 50s now, still playing. He runs the ex-Rams team that was founded in the 1960s by Tim Ward and which has raised thousands of pounds for charity over the years. Like Kevin Hector, his playing partner in the second championship team in 1974-75, he doesn't look much different. Hector still plays, too, and occasionally, almost like the re-run of a film, images return of the glory, glory days.

Although he was only just coming up to his 21st birthday when he joined Derby County, Davies came into full-time professional football late. He didn't serve the apprenticeship at a League club like most players do, but came from non-League football. More than 25 years later, Malcolm Christie was to follow the same route. It doesn't happen very often and perhaps, because of that, the players themselves value the opportunity they've been given more highly. They know that the chance nearly slipped them by.

Davies joined Derby County from Worcester City in September 1971: "I think at the time it was a record transfer fee for a non-League player, £14,000, from Worcester City. I'd only played a few games for them, actually, and Peter Taylor had been to watch me play a few times. I did well when I went there. I think I scored seven goals in three games for Worcester City. It was the first time I'd ever been paid for playing football, for Worcester City. I thought you played football for enjoyment and when someone starts paying you for it, I thought it was absolutely brilliant, getting money for playing football."

In his first season at Derby, Davies played in the Reserves team that won the Central League title. The following year he made his Football League debut, but not for Derby County. He was loaned to Preston North End and played his first game against Queen's Park Rangers. He played a few games for Preston before requesting a return to Derby. Brian Clough obliged and gave him his Derby County debut in the Texaco Cup Final, against Airdrieonians, in which he scored. His League debut was away to Manchester City in November 1972. Derby County lost, 4-0.

In the latter part of that 1972-73 season, Davies played more regularly. He made 19 League appearances and scored nine goals, but he really hit the headlines in the FA Cup fourth-round replay at Tottenham. A crowd of 52,736 crammed into White Hart Lane to see Spurs take a 3-1 lead after 78 minutes. Two minutes later, Davies pulled one back and with four minutes left, he scored again, a magnificent volley from a tight angle. In the second half of extra-time, Davies completed his hat-trick and Hector added another for a sensational 5-3 victory. Later that season came the European Cup semi-final. In a controversial match in Turin, amidst allegations that the German referee had been 'got at' by Juventus's German midfielder Helmut Haller at half-time, the Rams lost 3-1. Davies missed that match, but played in the second-leg at the Baseball Ground. McFarland and Gemmill were absent after being harshly booked in the first leg, Hinton missed a penalty and Davies was sent off. The result was a 0-0 draw. Brian Glanville of *The Sunday Times* then instigated an investigation which claimed that the Portuguese referee, Lobo, had been bribed to make sure the Italians didn't lose. It was all a long way from Worcester City.

Davies was a proper centre-forward. Tall – around 6ft 3ins in height – long-backed like a guardsman, he had good control and held the ball up well in the O'Hare tradition. He must have been awkward to play against, but good to play with and he was a regular member of the second championship side. In March of that 1974-75 season, he scored all five goals in a 5-0 win over Luton Town and finished with 12 goals in 39 games. He made 98 League appearances in his first spell for Derby County and scored 31 goals, before signing for Bruges in August 1975. He helped them to win a Belgium League and Cup double before joining Leicester City for a season. He then played in America, but returned for a short spell at Derby before returning to the States. He also had a brief spell at Darlington. Overall, he made 144 appearances for Derby County, plus 22 as substitute and scored 44 goals. Most of all, he enjoyed playing.

Bobby Davison – sharp as a tack

BOBBY Davison was sharp as a tack. A loose ball in the penalty area, a blur of navy blue and white and that ball nestling cosily in the net. Neat and tidy was Davison. 'Bright' in the current coaching jargon. He headed the Rams' list of goalscorers in League matches in each of the five seasons between 1983 and 1987 and his 106 goals in 246 appearances, plus three as substitute, in all competitions, puts him tenth in Derby County's all-time goalscorers' list. More than that, he was good to watch and could surely have played at the top level in any era.

Centre-forwards come in all shapes and sizes. Davison was more Gary Lineker than Alan Shearer. Quick moving and alert, he had good anticipation, real sharpness off the mark and a predatory instinct for goals. True speed is 'being there'. Davison had that quality. Of Jimmy Greaves, Geoffrey Green wrote in *The Times*: 'He was the Fagin of the penalty area; the arch pickpocket of goals.' There was a bit of that about Davison, although this most self-depreciating of forwards would certainly have been embarrassed to be compared with a master craftsman like Greaves.

There was more to Davison's game, however, than just scoring goals. He led the line, could receive and hold the ball as well as most and he provided a focal point at the front of the team. Not the biggest centre-forward around, he nevertheless won his fair share in the air and like most good players he could ride a tackle. Perhaps, like Kevin Hector, his biggest asset was good balance. Not often was Davison on the floor and, like Hector, he stayed fit. Between September 1983 and December 1985 he recorded a run of 126 consecutive appearances, which especially for a forward, is an excellent record.

He was signed by Peter Taylor from Halifax Town in 1982 and saw Derby County through successive promotions under Arthur Cox before he left to join Leeds United in 1987. It nearly didn't happen though. He nearly joined Arsenal. He went on loan at Highbury for a month whilst at Halifax Town, but after ten days, Peter Taylor got wind of what was happening and approached Halifax with a bid. Terry Neill was the Arsenal manager and told Davison that Arsenal wanted to sign him and that they would match the Rams' offer to Halifax. It was up to him. Two things persuaded Davison to sign for Derby County. First, Taylor suggested he would have a better chance of a first-team place at the Baseball Ground than at Highbury. Secondly, travelling in London was getting on his nerves. We can all appreciate that.

Davison led the Rams' attack brilliantly in season 1984-85, scoring 24 League goals, the most since Ray Straw's record 37 in 1956-57. Then, in November 1987, a chance to join Leeds United, then an average Second Division, for some reason proved too strong and he left during Derby County's first season back in the First Division. He returned, briefly, in 1991, on loan, scoring eight goals in ten games to give impetus and hope to Derby's Second Division season. He also recorded his 100th goal for the club. Not many players in Derby County's history have been more popular than Bobby Davison.

Peter Doherty – rebel with a cause

PETER Doherty played only 15 League matches for Derby County and 25 matches in all competitions, yet he is remembered as one of the truly 'great' players in the club's history. Raich Carter was adamant that Doherty was the best player he ever played with – which, being Raich, would mean the second best player ever – and their partnership at inside-forward had spectators drooling with pleasure. It was the foundation of Derby County's FA Cup Final victory of 1946.

Carter and Doherty did play for Derby County as 'guest' players during the war years, about 60 appearances each. They were in the RAF, stationed at Loughborough, and were brought over to the Baseball Ground by their squadron-leader, Dan Maskell, who became equally famous as a tennis commentator. In an article entitled 'Footballers at War', published in 1947, Doherty wrote about those wartime football experiences: 'When the Prime Minister announced that we were at war on that sunny September morning in 1939, most people realised that the whole fabric of their lives would probably be changed – and changed violently. For professional footballers, the cleavage was a harsh one; contracts were automatically torn up and for those players who had families to support and no savings to fall back on, the immediate prospect was grave. It was a grim lesson for professionals and one that some of us took to heart very seriously. Without a scrap of consideration or sentiment, our means of livelihood were simply jettisoned and we were left to find fresh ones as best we could.'

These actions left a lasting impression on Doherty, particularly the power of the clubs to retain control over players, despite having no responsibility to them.

Doherty was a courteous and polite individual, renowned for the help and encouragement he gave to youngsters, but he was dissatisfied with the system within football and the unfair treatment of players. The seeds of the idea to improve conditions – which, ultimately, led to the abolition of the maximum wage and freedom of contract for players – germinated with a number of strong-minded footballers like Peter Doherty.

Doherty was playing for Manchester City when war broke out: 'I applied to Leyland Motors and Vickers Armstrong, Manchester, for work, but without success. Then a friend in Scotland offered me a job at Greenock, and I accepted. My conscience was perfectly clear. As my contract had been broken, I considered myself a free agent and perfectly at liberty to find work where I chose. Football was clearly a secondary consideration and my family responsibilities were my main concern. I would no longer be available for City and I informed the club to this effect. Mr Smith, the City chairman, was not quite so sympathetic as he had been when I signed. "I have been informed by Mr Wild that you are going to Scotland," he said. "Is that true?" I replied that it was. "I don't want you to be under any misapprehension," he went on, "but you won't play any football in Scotland." Because I couldn't turn out for City, I was to be barred from playing with a Scottish club on free Saturday afternoons! We seemed to be getting all the kicks and none of the ha'pence, and I told the chairman so'.

It was the start of a battle of wills, throughout the war years, between Doherty and Manchester City. A major objection was being ordered to play for certain clubs: 'Once again, in spite of the fact that all contracts had been cancelled, I was receiving orders as if I were a full-time player getting a normal weekly wage. I hadn't the slightest objection to playing for West Brom, and I told Mr Everiss, the secretary, so. But I did think I should have some say in the matter of the clubs for whom I played.'

Doherty left Derby County for Huddersfield Town in December 1946. He was sad: "I would have been happy to have ended my days at Derby. But the directors felt that my plans to take over the Arboretum Hotel near the ground would affect my game. All I can say is they did not know me." He was labelled 'a militant troublemaker', but those people who did know, spoke of him with genuine affection. Undoubtedly, he was 'a players' player'. In The Who's Who of Derby County, Peter Doherty is described as 'a football trade unionist ahead of his time'.

Dally Duncan – wonderful left foot

"THE art of wing play is to have a definite idea of what you intend to do with the ball, presuming things go all right." So said Billy Meredith, who played for Manchester City and Manchester United in the early part of the century, was an early campaigner for the removal of the maximum wage and laid the foundations of the Professional Footballers' Association. He should know. The idiosyncratic Welsh winger, who always played with a toothpick in his mouth, was recalled to play in an FA Cup quarter-final in 1924, when he was 50 years old!

 Dally Duncan didn't last quite that long, although he was the oldest member of the 1946 FA Cup-winning team and when he played his last match for Derby County on 28 September 1946 – the same day as Sammy Crooks – he was 37 years of age. He was transferred to Luton Town as player-coach, then took over as player-manager and he finally retired from playing in 1948. He was the first of the FA Cup winners to leave Derby County.

Mark Hooper and Ellis Rimmer (Sheffield Wednesday), Ernie Toseland and Eric Brook (Manchester City), Joe Hulme and Cliff Bastin (Arsenal), Albert Geldard and Jimmy Stein (Everton) were the wing partnerships from which many of the goals scored by centre-forwards like Dixie Dean and Ted Drake emanated. The 1930s was an era when wingers hunted in pairs and scoring goals was the main aim of the game. In season 1930-31, three teams – Arsenal, Aston Villa and Sheffield Wednesday – scored more than 100 goals in Division One. Derby County scored a mere 94.

That scoring rate didn't last, but wingers were still an essential part of any team and after Duncan joined Derby County in 1932, the names Crooks and Duncan became inseparable They even appeared on opposing teams in international matches. 'Sammy' and 'Dally' supporters called them, with that measure of familiarity and the use of the first name accorded to particular favourites.

If Crooks was swift and direct, Duncan was of a different style. "Dally was clever with it, but he wasn't the forceful type. You wouldn't see him go and knock a full-back over or anything like that, but he'd got a lot of skill had Dally," said Tommy Powell. "He was so graceful. A bit similar to Alan Hinton, but more graceful."

He played in 289 matches for Derby County and scored 69 goals, a healthy rate for a winger, and he made 14 appearances for Scotland. "Wonderful left foot. Wonderful dribbler, said Roy Christian. "Compared to Sammy he looked big, but he wasn't really. He was broader. I would think he was about 5ft 9in or 5ft 10ins, something like that, whereas Sammy was 5ft 6ins. Less of a winger's build than Sammy, but Dally scored some good goals. They were mostly from the wing; he very rarely cut in, but he could swerve the ball, which not many people could do in those days."

After a period at Luton Town as manager, Duncan went to manage Blackburn Rovers and led them to the 1960 FA Cup Final where they lost 3-0 to Wolves, after Dave Whelan, now the multi-million pounds owner of JJB Sports, was carried off in the first half with a broken leg.

Alf Jeffries played for Derby County in the late 1930s: "Lovely footballer was Dally. Tight as a duck's bottom. Wouldn't give anything away. Wouldn't give a thing away. I don't suppose he gave a penny for a flag. He finished up on the south coast at Brighton in a hotel. He died down there. Good footballer, mind."

Alan Durban – always there

'SPEED is being there'. On the training ground, Alan Durban was slow. On the pitch, he was 'there'. He was there often enough to score 133 League goals in a career of 15 years that spanned 538 full League games, plus 16 as a substitute. For Derby County, he played a total of 388 matches, plus 15 as a substitute and scored 112 goals. Essentially a midfield player, Durban's scoring record was tremendous. Being there was his secret; timing was the key. Running speed had very little to do with it. Like it was said of Kenny Dalglish: 'The first three yards were in his head.'

Durban joined Derby County from Cardiff City in 1963. "I just got a 'phone call, about a fortnight before pre-season training, to say that they'd agreed a fee with Derby." Negotiations didn't take long in that era. "I think I'd gone from something like £12 and £10, to something like £20 and £18, which was a monstrous rise for me at that stage. I said 'yes' within, probably, an hour, jumped on the train and went back to my Mum and Dad. Funny isn't it? I mean, nowadays, they're on mobile phones, asking for advice from all quarters, but there I was, just 21 years old. I just got on the train and went to Derby. Went in the office for an hour, decided in my own mind: 'Yeah, I think it will be good for me.' And left."

Durban usually knew his own mind. The Derby County dressing-room, especially in the championship days, had some strong minded individuals who had confidence in their own ability, although Durban signed for Derby County long before the arrival of Brian Clough. He was another of the shrewd signings made by previous manager Tim Ward. Others included Eddie Thomas, a goalscoring inside-forward, who with Durban and centre-forward Ian Buxton provided plenty of goals in the Second Division in the mid-1960s. Unfortunately, Derby County's defence also conceded plenty of goals. Ward's solution was interesting. Durban reflects, "The funny thing is, you'd have thought we wanted defenders, the goals that we let in, but Tim went and bought Kevin [Hector]. Tim was a creative player himself and he wanted a nice 'slide-rule pass' team, wanted goalscorers, and if you look, we bought very few defenders. He kept buying creative players, rather than others." Ian Buxton looks back, "I remember a match at Birmingham under Tim Ward and we actually drew 5-5! Fancy playing away from home and drawing five-each. I can't tell you what was said afterwards to the defence, by the forwards. Like all matches like that you get in the dressing room and...!"

Then came Clough. "No, no, I didn't take to Cloughie straightaway," says Durban. "No, he was a pain in the arse, a pain in the arse. Why? Because he stopped us playing golf and things, all of a sudden. Peter Daniel was always going back to work on the farm; Webber was always going back farming; me and Saxo used to spend a bit of time in the betting shop and so on – we all had other interests. I think that the other interests, at times, overtook our jobs. At the time we didn't realise it, but then, all of a sudden, he came in and very, very, quickly changed our thinking, so that we were focussed completely on the job."

Durban became focussed on the job to the extent that he became an integral part of the Derby County rise to the top under Clough and Peter Taylor. Second Division and First Division championship medals came his way and he played in the European Cup. He also won 27 Welsh international caps.

He left Derby in 1973 to become assistant player-manager and then manager at Shrewsbury Town. He managed Stoke City, Sunderland, where he signed a teenage Ally McCoist from St Johnstone, Cardiff City, and was assistant to manager Roy McFarland at Derby County. For several years he managed the National Tennis Centre at Telford. A county tennis player himself and a cricketer good enough to play for Glamorgan and Derbyshire 2nd XIs, Durban succeeded Ward as chairman of Derby County Former Players' Association.

The memory of Durban is clear as crystal. That jerky, high-knee, marionette-style of running, blond hair flopping, arms pumping, as he popped up in a crowded penalty area like a genie from a bottle, to nudge another goalscoring chance away. "Anyone can score from there" they'd say. So they could, if they were there.

Stefano Eranio – sheer quality

WHEN Stefano Eranio joined Derby County in May 1997 it marked an important moment in the club's history and development. Foreign players had played for Derby County before, including Egyptian inside-forward Tewfick Abdallah, who joined Derby County in season 1920-21 and played 15 games, scoring one goal, before leaving to join Cowdenbeath. Abdallah heard about the Rams when he played for the Egyptian Army against British soldiers in World War One and decided to try his luck in England afterwards. The story is that he arrived at the Baseball Ground with little knowledge of the English language. "Foot the ball," was about his limit to manager Jimmy Methven, who thought he wanted to watch the Rams play and spent some time trying to sell him a season ticket, before realisation struck. Abdallah preferred to play in bare feet, but soon adjusted to boots, was signed as a professional and earned the nickname 'Toothpick', because of his ability to dribble through defences. For a short time he was a popular figure with the Baseball Ground regulars. More recently, Igor Stimac, Aljosa Asanovic, Mart Poom, Paulo Wanchope, Francesco Baiano and Fabrizio Ravanelli have been the most prominent of Derby County's foreign imports, but even Abdallah couldn't have been more popular with Derby supporters than Eranio.

He came to Derby County on a Bosman free transfer from AC Milan, which was significant for two reasons. First, the Bosman Ruling, which allows players to move freely at the end of their contracts and without a transfer fee being involved, was in its infancy and this was Derby County's first major venture into its benefits. Secondly, AC Milan are one of the really big clubs of European football, having won the European Cup five times and been in three other Finals. They were also three-times winners of the World Club Championship and for a player with more than 20 Italian international caps to come to Derby County from a club of such international repute was something that had not happened before.

As to be expected, Eranio brought sheer quality. Initially played at right-wing-back, later in a more central midfield role, Eranio was able to influence games by his confidence in supporting the attack and his control and skill in possession. Some of the football played in Derby County's first season at Pride Park, in 1997-98, brought back reminders of the neat style and accurate passing of the championship years at the Baseball Ground, as Eranio, compatriot Francesco Baiano, and Paulo Wanchope linked effectively at the front, whilst Igor Stimac and Chris Powell provided authority and calm distribution from the back. Derby County finished in ninth position in that season and eighth the following year, in 1998-99. There's no substitute for skill.

Unfortunately, Baiano, Stimac and Wanchope went their separate ways leaving Eranio the sole survivor of the quartet. Other players also moved on and Derby County began to struggle as the replacements were unable to match the previous levels of skill and ability. The club finished finished successively, 16th and 17th.

At the end of season 2000-2001, it looked as though Eranio's career at Derby County was over after 108 appearances, including 83 in the Premiership, plus 12 as a substitute. The club declined his request in January, to give a definite answer regarding a future contract, so because of concerns about his two daughters' education – to be schooled back in Italy they had to be registered months ahead – Eranio decided to leave Derby County. Ironically, in the final two months of the season he played some of his most effective football for the club, culminating in a splendid display in the penultimate match of the season, when Derby County beat Manchester United 1-0 at Old Trafford to confirm their place in the Premiership. In the final match, at home to Ipswich, Eranio bade an emotional farewell to the fans.

Nothing is sure in football. In the close season, Eranio played a part in smoothing certain aspects of Fabrizio Ravanelli's transfer to Pride Park. Then, having failed to find a suitable club in Italy, the 33-year-old Eranio found himself on a plane back to Derby and signing a further one-year deal to play for Derby County. 'Never go back', they say. Of course, Eranio had never really been away.

Marco Gabbiadini – an enigma

THEY called him 'Marco Goalo' at Sunderland. Alan Smith, assistant manager at Crystal Palace, shortly after Gabbiadini was transferred to Selhurst Park, labelled him 'a distinctly average player'. Both views, in their way, were correct. Gabbiadini was somewhat of an enigma, doing splendid things one minute, clumsy and crude things the next. He excited and infuriated Rams supporters in equal measure, and consistency was never his strongest suite. After arriving for £1 million from Crystal Palace, he had a chequered career at the Baseball Ground, being voted Player of the Year at the end of his first season, but jeered from the terraces at other times. Even so, he made 200 appearances for Derby County and scored 68 goals.

He was signed by manager Arthur Cox in January 1992. It was the start of the massive spending spree, backed by new owner Lionel Pickering, which was designed to propel Derby County into the First Division, which effectively became the Premier League the following season. Within a short period, other big-money signings like Paul Simpson, Paul Kitson, and Tommy Johnson arrived. Later, Mark Pembridge, Craig Short, Martin Kuhl, Gary Charles and John Harkes took the total spending to over £12 million, but the plan didn't work. Football is played on the pitch, not on a balance sheet. The idea of buying young players of potential so that, if necessary, any money spent can be recouped at a later date, is dependent on an accurate judgment of a player's ability in the first place. Despite supporters being told repeatedly by the club that 'these are good players', the plain truth was that Pickering's money was being wasted. The players bought were not and never were, good enough. Neither was the team.

Gabbiadini was an experienced player by the time he arrived at the Baseball Ground, with 281 appearances and 112 goals in his locker. He scored on his debut, a 1-0 win at Portsmouth, with a low angled first-time drive, which gave promise of better things to come. By the end of the season, the Rams were in the play-offs, but lost 5-4 on aggregate to Blackburn Rovers.

Gabbiadini could be a very exciting player at times. Very strong in the legs, with a low centre of gravity, he was quite sharp off the mark, hard to shift and was a good striker of the ball with his right foot. His strength was his strength. Partly because of that, he didn't get injured much. On some days he held the ball up nicely, on others the wretched thing bounced about all over the place and possession was lost cheaply. He also looked always to run with the ball, whenever he received it. Such a style catches the eye, but to succeed like George Best, there is always a time and place. Gabbiadini often got the time and place in the wrong order, much to the chagrin of colleagues, supporters and, no doubt, management, but, on the other hand, no-one could be certain he wouldn't pop up with a spectacular goal. Over a long and successful career, particularly in the lower echelons of the game, from York City to Northampton Town, via Sunderland, Crystal Palace, Derby County, Greece and Darlington, Marco 'Goalo' Gabbiadini often did.

Hughie Gallacher – could make a ball talk

LIFE is often about ups and downs, interspersed with moments of elation and distress. Hughie Gallacher had more than a helping of both. He is recognised universally as one of the all-time 'greats' of British football, but his life ended in tragedy.

Despite their claims of being a 'big club', the last time Newcastle won the League championship was in 1927 and Gallacher was captain. He was also at centre-forward in the wonderful 'Wee Wembley Wizards' who beat England 5-1 in 1928. In that same Scotland team was Alex James, who went to Bellshill Academy in Glasgow, as did Gallacher.

Gallacher was married at 17 and divorced at 20 and by the time he arrived at Derby, aged 32, his reputation was firmly established, both on and off the field. Part of the £2,750 transfer fee George Jobey paid Chelsea to sign Gallacher in 1934 was for the purpose of paying off debts incurred by the player. Gallacher was well known to favour a drop of the hard stuff and a flutter on the horses, but it didn't seem to affect his playing performances unduly. On his debut for the Rams, he scored within six minutes and he put all five in Blackburn Rovers' net in a 5-2 win at Ewood Park in the same season. In all, he made 55 appearances and scored 40 goals for Derby County and saw the Rams into second place in the League championship table in 1936. Then he was on his way again, to Notts County, in the autumn.

Small, 5ft 5ins in height, stocky and as hard as nails, Gallacher could look after himself on the field, but he also had great skill. Tommy Powell: "I saw Hughie Gallacher play. Tremendous. No bigger than two penn'oth of chips, but he could make a ball talk. Back to goal, I mean, he used to be so cheeky. He'd back-heel them here and there." Always, though, was the booze. Dally Duncan played with him: "Hughie Gallacher was a charming fellow, a different fellow altogether when he was sober." In the end, the drink probably killed him.

Sam Weaver, who won three England caps, played with Hughie Gallacher at Newcastle. Weaver was the first exponent of the long throw-in and was a member of Newcastle's FA Cup-winning team of 1932. Many years later, he was physiotherapist for Derbyshire County Cricket Club and reserve-team trainer at Mansfield Town. Sam believed Gallacher to be the best player he ever played with and talked of an era when more than 3,000 fans used to gather at the station at Newcastle, to welcome the team back after away matches, especially if they'd been successful in London.

Gallacher disliked the fuss and, besides, he usually had other things on his mind, possibly the proximity of closing time. Whatever the reason, special arrangements were always made to stop the London-Edinburgh express just before the Tyne Bridge at Gateshead, to allow Gallacher to get off.

Many years later, in June 1957, he was charged with cruelty to his 14-year-old son, Matthew. An incident had got out of hand and Gallacher had thrown an ashtray at the child, hitting him on the head. The boy was taken into care. The day before he was due to appear before Gateshead magistrates, Gallacher walked to Low Fell station near his home, climbed over a fence and jumped in front of the York-Edinburgh express. That morning he had posted a letter to the magistrates expressing regret. If he lived to be a hundred, he wrote, he'd never forgive himself for striking Matthew.

Hughie Gallacher was 54 years old when his decapitated body was removed from the railway line 100 yards from a spot known as Dead Man's Crossing.

Archie Gemmill – he was everywhere

WHEN Archie Gemmill first started pursuing the ball in Derby County's midfield, it was like watching a squirrel hunting for nuts. He was everywhere. Unfortunately, once he found what he was looking for, he ran with it ceaselessly. Even supporters were breathless. Fortunately, as he got older and wiser, his game matured until he became as complete a midfielder as there was in football. His passing improved immeasurably, both in quality and in timing, which was much to the benefit of colleagues and appreciation of spectators, whilst he never lost his energy, or his competitive outlook. More than anything, Gemmill was an irritant; an angry wasp. He never left opponents alone, never gave them any peace. It really had to be hard work, playing against Archie Gemmill, especially in the Baseball Ground mud.

"When he was running on heavy grounds, his feet were that quick, they only touched the surface. He never looked heavy," said Alan Durban, speaking first of Kevin Hector and then of Gemmill. "When Archie, who was exactly the same, came they could run over the top of it. It didn't matter how heavy it was. We're talking about us others being six inches down, while those two ran on the top."

Gemmill was another of those audacious Brian Clough and Peter Taylor signings that wasn't without a touch of controversy. Gemmill had won Scottish under-23 honours at Preston North End, and Everton were known to want to sign him. Derby County were not mentioned at all. Alan Ball was an Everton player at the time and it just happened that his father, Alan Ball senior, was manager of Preston. It seemed a formality that Gemmill would go to Merseyside. Clough and Taylor had other ideas, aided by a tip-off from new Derby County secretary, Stuart Webb, who had just left his position as assistant secretary at Preston North End. Gemmill was due to sign for Everton one Monday. Instead, he found himself on the way to Derby, after having had Clough stay overnight at the family home.

It's sometimes forgotten that Gemmill captained the side in the second championship success, because Roy McFarland was injured for all but the final four matches. He was one of eight Rams players to appear in both championship-winning teams and he then went off to win a third championship medal at Nottingham Forest, although was left out of the 1979 European Cup Final team. He also played 43 times for Scotland and will always be remembered for that stunning dribble in which he left three Dutch defenders bemused, on his way to scoring the goal of the tournament in the 1978 World Cup Finals in Argentina. How he must be tired of being asked about that.

Like other Derby County championship winners Kevin Hector, Bruce Rioch and Roy McFarland, Gemmill returned for another spell at his former club, in 1982, but it didn't become a re-run of former glories. After all his previous success at the Baseball Ground, he was a member of the Derby County side relegated to Division Three in 1984. Overall, he made 404 appearances for Derby and didn't get injured very much. He scored 33 goals. Alan Hinton, with a nice line in Americanisms, summed up his energetic style: "I mean, Gemmill was like an athlete you'd never seen before. He was up and down that field like a horse. I mean, he was fantastic."

Charlie George – he just hit it

CHARLIE George is one of those rare footballers who became a folk hero at more than one club. From the terraces of the North Bank at Highbury, where he grew up as a fan of Arsenal, to the heights of playing in the European Cup for Derby County on memorable floodlit evenings, Charlie George attracted a following like the Pied Piper of Hamlyn. No Arsenal player, before or since, has been more popular than Charlie. No former Derby County player, when he reappears at Pride Park and previously, the Baseball Ground, to attend a function or present an award, ever gets a greater ovation than the player who touched genius with his talent and yet has always retained the common touch. These days he spends part of his time hosting guests at Highbury on match days. Watching him greet them is fascinating. Well-known celebrities, captains of industry, groups of awe-struck children, all come to the Charlie George Suite in the Clock Stand. Rich and poor, Charlie treats them all the same. They love the Pied Piper. Charlie George, a living legend? Undoubtedly.

It wasn't always so. In his youthful years he had a reputation for being unruly. Long lank hair, shirt outside his shorts and flashes of temper were not attributes which endeared him to officialdom. There was also an air of menace about him which fitted conveniently with some attitudes that prevailed on the terraces in football's most violent era. George was, for a time, a popular icon with the less savoury elements around the game and he was no angel. In *Fever Pitch*, Nick Hornby writes: 'On my birthday in 1971, shortly before his goal against Newcastle, one of the frequent red mists that plagued him had descended and he had grabbed a rugged Newcastle defender by the throat and lifted him from the ground. This was not misfit petulance, this was hard-man menace, and the likely lads on the terraces have never had a more convincing representative.'

A two-finger sign to the Main Stand at the Baseball Ground, when he scored the second Arsenal goal in a 2-2 draw in February 1972, didn't help public relations either, but by the time he joined Derby County in 1975, he had mellowed somewhat.

Don't the images come flooding back? Lying on his back at Wembley, arms raised, the ball nestling in the back of Liverpool's net after a thunderous right-foot shot shot beat Ray Clemence high to his right hand, won the FA Cup for Arsenal and sealed the 'double' in 1971. It was one of the most famous goals in the history of the Arsenal club and one of the most dramatic photographs. Then there was the half-volley, swept in against Real Madrid at a throbbing Baseball Ground under October floodlights in 1975, as Derby County dismantled the Spanish giants 4-1 and George scored a hat-trick. Says George, "The goal in the Madrid game was a good move. It went from left to right and then back again. When it came back to me, I just hit and it went in. Sometimes they do and sometimes they finish in the crowd." Sometimes they live in the memory, like as if yesterday.

In the wider football world, Charlie George is largely associated with Arsenal, like Francis Lee is with Manchester City and Raich Carter with Sunderland, but George actually made more League starts for the Rams than he did for the Gunners. He was signed for Derby County by Dave Mackay in July 1975, after the Rams had won their second championship. He had an important observation about that side: "The thing that struck me immediately was was the way they played it out from the back. That's what I noticed straight away. It was different to what I'd been used to." He did have one regret: "I was a little disappointed I didn't win anything at Derby because I thought they they were a real quality side. I was fortunate to play with them and scored some important goals."

It is sometimes forgotten that George also played for Southampton and that Brian Clough signed him for Nottingham Forest in 1979. He also played two matches for Bournemouth, before returning for a second, albeit brief, spell at the Baseball Ground in 1982, when he added 11 more League appearances to the 106 he made in his first spell. In total he played 147 games for Derby County, scored 56 goals and played just once for England.

Archie Goodall – footballer and showman

ARCHIE Goodall was the younger of the the two Goodall brothers who between them played more than 650 matches for Derby County in the late 19th and early 20th centuries. The sons of a soldier who was posted all over Britain, they were opposites in many ways. Archie, born in Belfast but raised in Scotland, was a rumbustuous centre-half with a stubborn streak, who played for several clubs like Liverpool Stanley (and including a few games for the Rams) before the Football League was formed in 1888. Then he played for Preston North End and Aston Villa, his transfer between the two in October 1888 being the first to be approved by the new League, before he joined Derby County in May 1889. He played five times for Ireland, being the first player with an English club to do so. John Goodall, a year older, was an outstanding forward who played 14 times for England, but was of an entirely different temperament.

Archie Goodall was a tough, strong individual, who with 151 appearances easily holds the Derby County record of consecutive appearances in League matches. In achieving that figure, in a five-year period between December 1892 and September 1897, Goodall didn't miss a single match in any competition, an unbroken run of 167 competitive matches. A total of 380 League appearances puts him ninth on the Derby County all-time list. His total of 42 appearances is third for the FA Cup.

He played in the days when a centre-half was the fulcrum of the team, defending, but also attacking. Such was that particular style of play, it's probable that centre-halves were more akin to modern midfield players than to the stopper centre-half that developed with Herbert Chapman's Arsenal teams of the 1930s and became the norm in modern football. As a result of his attacking role, Goodall scored 52 goals in his career for Derby County, many of which were described as being from 'strong shots'.

An early indication of Goodall's outlook on life was that after initially agreeing to the transfer from Villa to Derby County, he tried to back out of the arrangement, but once that was smoothed over he proceeded to miss only one game in his first season. That, interestingly, was when refused to play at Preston, claiming his wife was ill.

He played in the team that finished runners-up in Division One in 1895-96 and in the FA Cup Final teams of 1897-98 (lost 3-1 to Nottingham Forest) and 1902-03 (lost 6-0 to Bury, still a record defeat in an FA Cup Final). Before the 1898 Final, played at the Crystal Palace, Goodall was spotted outside the ground trying to sell tickets, which he had bought as an 'investment'. The FA did not bring any charges. He was unfit to play in the 1898-99 Final (lost 4-1 to Sheffield United), although he played in three of the earlier Cup rounds and made 26 appearances, out of a possible 34, in the League season. He also refused to play extra-time in a United Counties Cup game on the last day of one season, claiming that his contract had expired at the end of 90 minutes.

Football was not his only sport. He played cricket, was a keen follower of country sports and surprised several professional strongmen in contests of strength. He could raise 150lbs with one hand and 184lbs overhead with two and when he retired from football, he toured Europe and America with with a strongman's act, which featured him 'walking around a metal hoop' which he had built in a shed at his Wolfa Street, Derby, home. Times change.

John Goodall – Nature's gentleman

JOHN Goodall was the elder by one year and the less flamboyant of the two brothers who played for Derby County in the late 19th and early 20th centuries. He played in a variety of forward positions, mostly centre-forward, and was capped by England on 14 occasions for, despite being brought up in Scotland and having Irish parents, he was born in London.

John Goodall joined Derby County from Preston North End in May 1889. He was a member of the Preston team that became known as 'the Old Invincibles' by doing the double of League champions and FA Cup winners in the first season the Football League was formed, in 1888. Preston had the League won by January and didn't lose a match all season, whilst in the FA Cup they beat Wolverhampton Wanderers 3-0 in the Final, played at Kennington Oval cricket ground. John Goodall was such a big name that when he signed, the Derby secretary went round the town sticking up posters to announce the fact.

Derby County was formed in 1884 and in the first match the club ever played, John Goodall scored five goals. Unfortunately, they weren't for the Rams. They were scored for Great Lever, a team from near Bolton, for which he was making his debut. Great Lever won the match 6-0, to gave Derby County an inauspicious start in football life.

Steve Bloomer was in no doubt as to his value to the club and to himself. He wrote: 'Johnny Goodall was a wonderful footballer, brilliant captain and Nature's gentleman, but little did I think when all the fuss was made over his arrival from Preston what an influence for good was being brought into my life. As my early mentor he talked to me and passed on his learnings... straight to the point he told you what to do and expected it to be done and I always maintain that no player has ever known as much about football and its methods and policies than this old friend of mine. The two fundamentals he passed on to me were complete ball control and an ability to think a moment ahead of the other fellow. Times without number he impressed that upon me, to think all the time the game was in progress, even when play was not actually near me. There is nothing better than being taken under the wing of an old player and I had the additional slice of luck of being endowed with a temperament which allowed me to enjoy my football lessons with relish. I'm sure I owe more to John Goodall than to anybody else for my ultimate success on the football field.'

Goodall captained the Rams team which finished Division One runners-up in 1895-96 and were beaten FA Cup Finalists in 1897-98 and in all, played 238 games for Derby County, scoring 85 goals. He left in 1899, to play for New Brighton Tower and Glossop.

He played cricket in two matches for Derbyshire, in 1895 and 1896, and later played for Hertfordshire. He was also a club champion at bowls and curling and was capable of century breaks at billiards, which he probably practised a bit when, along with brother Archie, he kept the Plough, near The Spot, on London Road. He also ran a sports shop in Babington Lane. His nickname 'Johnny All-Good' was reinforced when he saved a man from drowning in the River Derwent.

Les Green – agile, athletic, strong

SOME people say that the 1968-69 Derby County team that won promotion from Division Two, under Brian Clough and Peter Taylor, was the best Derby County team of all. They mean that if that team played any other Derby County team, of any era, it would win. Well, it's a good debating point. What is quite certain is that any team having even a slight claim to such high consideration must have a good goalkeeper. It was especially true of a team under the management of Clough and Taylor, who valued goalkeepers very highly.

For two seasons, Les Green was as good as any goalkeeper in the country, but if his career at the Baseball Ground was sweet while it lasted, it was also short. From his debut onwards, he made 129 consecutive appearances, 107 in the League, which was a tribute to his form in that period. Then he was dropped, after a calamitous display in a 4-4 draw against Manchester United, on Boxing Day 1970, and he never played for Derby County again. Having arrived to take over from Reg Matthews, Green found himself replaced by Colin Boulton, who had himself been signed originally by Tim Ward, to replace Matthews. Green's Derby County career was over.

Clough and Taylor knew all about Green when they signed him from Rochdale in May 1968. When Taylor was manager of Burton Albion he signed Green from Nuneaton Borough and then when Taylor joined Clough at Hartlepools, Green soon followed. He was sold to Rochdale in April 1967 following a disagreement about matters off the field – a sure way to find yourself on the transfer list under the Clough style of management – but when it was decided that Matthews was at the end of his career and Boulton was lacking experience, Green was forgiven. Taylor always put great emphasis on a goalkeeper's ability to organise a defence from the back and Green was particularly adept in that respect, if not a little idiosyncratic at times.

Like Harry Hibbs, Ron Springett, Alan Hodgkinson and Eddie Hopkinson, all England goalkeepers of renown, at 5ft 9ins Green wasn't very tall for a goalkeeper. "Although I was one of the shortest goalkeepers to play for Derby, height was less important in those days – we had positional sense. You could have taken any First Division 'keeper from that era and they could have played for the England team. It wasn't just about size and power, you had to be in the right position at the right time," he said. Green may not have been tall but he was wonderfully agile, athletic and strong. He was capable of terrific reflex saves and won 'Save of the Season' in BBC's *Match of the Day* awards, for a tremendous flying effort against Chelsea at Stamford Bridge in 1969.

After leaving Derby, Green went to play for Durban City in South Africa, but he suffered a badly broken leg which ended his career. He returned to live in Nuneaton and became manager of Nuneaton Borough in the early 1990s. Les Green and Derby County? Short, but sweet.

John Gregory – dictated the game

IT was no surprise that John Gregory went into football management when his playing days were over. When he was a player he managed things on the field. "I think he led by the way he played, not as much by what he said," says Eric Steele. "He was a deep thinker. He was a good captain on the field, because – I think Arthur [Cox] knew as well – we could put things right on the field ourselves, which is something, we say, is lacking in the modern game now. You look at the successful three, or four, sides. They've got people on the field, when they cross the white line, if it isn't going right, they can put it right. I can remember 'Gregs' in certain games, if we were overrun, we wouldn't look to Arthur, or Roy [McFarland], 'Gregs' would sort it out, midfield: 'You stay with him for five minutes, you stay with him and I'm holding in here.' We'd just kill the game for ten minutes. That was the sort of player he was."

Gregory had a proper apprenticeship in football. He played around 200 matches for Northampton Town, in five years, before being transferred to Aston Villa in 1977. After 59 League matches he joined Brighton and Hove Albion, where he made another 72 League appearances, some of which were at full-back. He then went to Queen's Park Rangers, in 1981. He appeared in their losing 1982 FA Cup Final team, against Tottenham Hotspur, and was an ever-present in the QPR team that won the Second Division championship in 1982-83. He joined Derby County, for £100,000, in November 1985 and became the 700th player in the club's history to play for the Rams.

Gregory was a neat passer of the ball, able to dictate the tempo of a game, and he had a lot of stamina. He was an elegant type of player, upright and controlled, but like Gary Micklewhite, he hadn't played in the lower divisions for nothing. "They came from Queen's Park Rangers and could be nasty," says Bobby Davison. "They could mix it with the best of players. Players now think: 'Gary Micklewhite? John Gregory? No, they wouldn't be hard men.' I'll tell you, they used to get stuck in."

Gregory was also a versatile player and appeared in nine different positions for Aston Villa. On a few occasions, he played in attack for Derby County, but it was in midfield where his influence was greatest, in the position where he won six England caps whilst with QPR. He complemented Geraint Williams in Derby County's midfield in the rise from the Third Division to the First Division in successive seasons under Arthur Cox. He played 124 matches for Derby County, plus one as substitute, and scored 23 goals, several with free-kicks from the edge of the penalty area.

Gregory left Derby County in 1988 to become player-coach and then manager for a year at Portsmouth. He moved to Plymouth to be caretaker-manager and then had a short spell at Bolton Wanderers before joining Leicester City as coach in June 1991. He left Leicester to succeed Martin O'Neill at Wycombe Wanderers and it was from Wycombe that he moved to Villa Park to become manager of Aston Villa. 'Billy Bigtime' his critics nicknamed him, initially, as he tried hard, too hard, to create an impression. He's settled down now, to become one of the more experienced managers in the game. His roots in football are deep. His father, also John, played nearly 200 matches for West Ham United, Scunthorpe United and Aldershot. Football is in his blood. John Gregory knows his way, very well, around the football world. Streetwise, you might say.

Reg Harrison – always laughing

"WHEN he laughs, everybody laughs," said Bert Mozley about Reg Harrison. Derby County can never have had a more popular player than the Derby-born right winger, who made such a fairytale appearance in the 1946 FA Cup Final. He's still laughing today. Harrison and Jimmy Bullions are the only two survivors of that legendary Cup-winning team and neither misses a match a Pride Park.

If enthusiasm for football was the only criteria for stardom, Harrison would have been one of the all-time 'greats'. His involvement with local clubs after his playing career was over, his coaching of youngsters in and around Derby ever since, plus his continued support of the club he supported from the terraces as a boy, earned him, in December 2000, the Derby County Former Players' Association Award of Merit. It's a rare honour. The inscription on the silver salver reads, 'For Services to Derby County and to Football.' To be recognised by one's peers is the highest accolade of all in football and only three people had been honoured previously, Jack Stamps, Raich Carter and Tommy Powell. It is a select list and Reg Harrison is a worthy addition.

Harrison had a hard act to follow at Derby County. Only Eddie Hapgood of Arsenal won more England caps between the two World Wars than Derby County's Sammy Crooks, who even played more times for England than Stanley Matthews in that period. Crooks was was Harrison's idol. In those days, every team had wingers, whose job it was to get down the outside of defenders and cross the ball for powerful centre-forwards who were good in the air, like Dixie Dean, Tommy Lawton and, at Derby, Jack Bowers and, later, Jack Stamps. Wingers tended to be of two types. Skilful dribblers, like Matthews and Dally Duncan, or quick, direct runners like Crooks and Harrison.

Although not a Crooks, Harrison was top-class material. He played 281 matches for Derby County and scored 59 goals, which was a good ratio for a winger. He was an ever present in 1951-52. In the League South game a week before the FA Cup Final, Harrison played at inside-right. That, too, was against Charlton Athletic, at The Valley. Crooks played on the right wing. He'd been injured in the second leg of the tie against Aston Villa at the Baseball Ground and Harrison had come into the team for the semi-final against Birmingham, managed by future Rams manager, Harry Storer. At Hillsborough, in front of a crowd of 65,000, the match ended 1-1. Harrison also played in the replay at Maine Road, which was watched by a crowd of 80,407. Derby County won 4-0 after extra-time and many people thought that Crooks would return for the Final. It was touch and go, but Harrison got the nod and, at Wembley, played well. "What a relief when we'd finished," said Harrison. "That we'd won. I can't remember much about it, really." It meant he was a Cup winner, before he'd played a Football League game, and it was the 12th match of the following season before he did so.

He left Derby County for Boston United after the 1954-55 season and returned as a member of the Boston team that beat Derby County 6-1 at the Baseball Ground in the second round of the FA Cup in 1955. It was an humiliating defeat and one of the big shocks in Cup history. "That was great," said Harrison. "I'd seen Albert Mays on the day of the second round draw, on the Monday. I was going towards Babbington Lane and he was coming the other way. He'd been up to the snooker hall and he saw me and said, 'Have you seen the draw? We'll thrash you.' I just grinned." Like Bert Mozley said, "When he laughs, everybody laughs."

Kevin Hector – that little bit extra

ALL players like being footballers, some actually like football. Kevin Hector just loved football. Playing football, I mean. He still does. If you happen to be passing a game on a local club's ground, or a park pitch somewhere around Derby, or more particularly, a charity game involving the Ex-Rams XI, spare a moment to have a look in and you may see a neat, well-balanced figure – who looks to be more in his mid-30s than his late 50s – moving effortlessly down the wing, or a little infield, with the ball close to his feet. The player and ball will be in complete harmony. It will look so simple, so economical, so smooth and so understated. That's how Kevin Hector played. That's how he was. He also scored goals.

Football supporters love a goalscorer. They especially love a goalscorer with style. "He was like a Rolls-Royce to a normal car. He just seemed to have a bit extra, Kevin," said Ron Webster. Rams' supporters initially welcomed him with open arms; they grew to value him enormously; ultimately, they adored him. Hector has long since passed into Derby County folklore and few players in the club's history will be remembered more fondly.

When Tim Ward signed him from Bradford Park Avenue in September 1966, it was like a bolt out of the blue. Not that Hector had suddenly appeared on the football scene. He'd already scored more than a century of goals for Bradford and appeared in nearly 200 matches (113 League goals: 176 League appearances) and as Alan Durban is apt to say, "He'd served his apprenticeship." His name had been linked with Manchester City, and other clubs were also said to interested. He wasn't unheard of in Derby, although few Rams fans would have seen him play. What really shook Derby County supporters was the size of the transfer fee. Around £40,000 was big money for a club trundling along in the old Second Division and reputedly unwilling to spend a bean. The immediate post-war years, when Derby County broke British record transfer fees, seemed long gone. So when it was announced that Derby County had signed Kevin Hector – for that amount of money – expectations were high. Hector didn't disappoint.

The impact was amazing. George Edwards wrote in the *Derby Evening Telegraph*: 'They cheered him off the pitch, then they waited half and hour and cheered him out of the ground, jostling to pat him on the back. And no wonder, for nobody could have asked more of a player on his debut than £40,000 Kevin Hector provided at the Baseball Ground on Saturday.' Huddersfield Town were beaten 4-3. Hector scored one of the goals. Durban scored a hat-trick, but few remember that. The rest, as they say, is history.

Kevin Hector heads the Derby County list of appearances, 581 plus eight as substitute and with 201 goals is second only to Steve Bloomer in the scorers' list. Amazingly, he missed only four League matches in seven seasons between 1967 and 1974. In 1975, when he won the second of his championship medals, he was absent for five games. It is not by accident supporters called him the 'King'. Hector played the game as it should be played, because he loved football dearly. Roy McFarland summed him up best: "...He wouldn't really say much, but when he said something everybody listened, because they knew it was important – and it was!"

Terry Hennessey – he played against Pele

IF ever you've got a few hours to spare, Terry Hennessey will tell you about the day he played against Pele. It was in the Maracana Stadium in Rio Di Janeiro, for Wales against Brazil. Hennessey's face will light up and his Welsh lilt will become even more pronounced as he recalls a point in the match when Pele approached him fairly slowly, with the ball at his feet. Hennessey thought he had all the avenues blocked and all the aces were his: "I knew there was no-one supporting him, so he had to take me on. Suddenly, he kicked the ball past me, as though he was passing it to someone else. I thought: 'Who's he passed that to?' Then he shot off like lightning and I realise the bugger had passed it to himself." He'll fall about laughing then, at the memory of playing against a genius like Pele.

Hennessey himself was a player of the highest class. Tall and prematurely bald, he was easily recognisable and was outstanding as an attacking wing-half with Birmingham City, before he joined Nottingham Forest in 1965. Brian Clough signed him in February 1970 and there were thoughts that he would replace Dave Mackay in defence. Mackay, of course, had other ideas, which meant Hennessey played in midfield as well as in defence, as Mackay played another full season before bowing out. The following season, 1971-72, Hennessey played in 17 matches (plus one as sub) as the championship was won with only 16 players. Of those 16, Tony Bailey made one appearance, Steve Powell two appearances (plus one sub), Jim Walker three appearances (plus three sub) and Frank Wignall ten appearances (plus one sub).

Hennessey was Derby County's first-ever £100,000 signing. It was an indication to everyone that the management meant business, but he was plagued by injury at the Baseball Ground and supporters never saw the best of him. He did play in both legs of the European Cup-tie against Benfica, being outstanding in the second leg in the Stadium of Light in Lisbon, where the Rams earned a 0-0 draw after beating Benfica 3-0 at the Baseball Ground. Although he played exactly 400 League matches in his career, he played only 79 matches (plus three as sub) in total for Derby County before the persistent and chronic knee injuries along with achilles tendon trouble, forced him to retire in 1973, aged 31.

After he retired, he managed Tamworth for a while. He even talked me out of retirement into playing for Tamworth for a season. Two crocks together, really. After a sojourn at Kimberley Town he went to America, to be assistant manager of Tulsa Roughnecks, before returning to manage Shepshed Charterhouse for a couple of years. He went back to America in 1980 for another stint with Tulsa and, later, Vancouver Whitecaps. Now he lives in Australia. I bet he's told the whole of Australia about the time he played against Pele.

Rob Hindmarch – a natural defender

THERE were no frills with Rob Hindmarch. What you saw was what you got with him. Big, strong, powerful and make no mistake, a centre-half from the day he was born. Hindmarch did what traditional centre-halves were supposed to do, defend first.

Hindmarch was signed by Arthur Cox from Sunderland in July 1984, two months after Cox was appointed manager of Derby County. It was no accident. Cox was assistant manager at Sunderland from 1973-76, when Hindmarch was an apprentice on his way to England Youth international honours. Hindmarch made his debut for Sunderland when he was a 17-year-old and, like Raich Carter many years before him, was captain of Sunderland as a teenager. He made 114 League appearances for the Rokerites and it was something of a surprise that he was allowed to leave Roker Park on a free transfer, despite the fact that he had a brief loan spell at Portsmouth earlier in the season.

Cox appointed him captain of Derby County at the start of the 1985-86 season and he led the Rams from the Third Division to the First Division in successive seasons. Some of the success of that team was due to the good spirit which existed between the players. Eric Steele says, "There was a great spirit. We used to go out and it was sensible. We'd go out on a Wednesday night every fortnight and we'd meet in a local hostelry and everybody would turn up. We didn't all drink and at the end of it, some would go for a meal, some would go home and it was brilliant and you'd be scared not to go. Now Arthur Cox didn't do that. What Arthur Cox did was to bring the players in and we generated our own spirit amongst us and we had some characters."

In total, Hindmarch made 196 appearances for Derby County and scored ten goals, including the only goal against Second Division Sheffield United in an excellent FA fourth-round Cup-tie on a frozen pitch, when a contingent of around 10,000 Derby County supporters made the trip and created a splendid atmosphere at Bramall Lane. Unfortunately, the Cup magic deserted the Rams. Another trip to Sheffield in the next round, this time to Hillsborough, saw them beaten 2-0 by First Division Sheffield Wednesday.

For much of his time at Derby, Hindmarch was partnered in central defence by Ross MacLaren. It was good pairing and in that first promotion season, Derby County conceded only 41 goals in 46 matches. Strong in the air, a bit ponderous on the floor, Hindmarch was generally the one who attacked the high ball down the middle and MacLaren picked up the pieces. MacLaren was quite accomplished in possession and was an ever-present in both promotion seasons, whilst Hindmarch missed only seven and nine matches respectively, because of injury.

Back in Division One, Hindmarch played the first three matches of the new campaign, but his days as an automatic choice at Derby were numbered. Fuelled by Robert Maxwell's money, Cox bought Mark Wright from Southampton and Hindmarch was relegated to the sidelines. He did reappear towards the end of February and Wright, who made a less than an assured start at Derby, benefited from having the big man alongside him. Cox kept reverting to Hindmarch – 25 League appearances in 1988-89, 26 in 1989-90 – until in June 1990, his contract ended, Hindmarch joined Wolverhampton Wanderers for a fee of £300,000. His time at Molineux was not a happy one and after a couple of seasons he left for pastures new and finally went to America. Few would say that Derby County didn't have good value from Rob Hindmarch.

Alan Hinton – a different kind of courage

WHITE boots. Long before David Beckham arrived on the scene, a Derby County player who played wide on the wing and scored some thunderous goals from free-kicks, who was as accurate with his passing and as deadly with his centres as Beckham is today, wore white boots. His name was Alan Hinton and he became one of Derby County's favourite sons, but it wasn't always thus. When he first arrived, he was taunted and teased. "Gladys, where's yer handbag?" they used to shout, as Hinton danced out of the way of a 50-50 confrontations with violent defenders of the 'Chopper' Harris, or Peter Storey mould. It needed some serious educating of the masses, by manager Brian Clough and assistant Peter Taylor, to convince supporters that Hinton would become the 'real deal'. Eventually, he did.

Hinton says, "I wasn't known for tackling and winning the ball, but the day it stopped – the players of Derby County saying he doesn't win the ball and all this stuff – was when Peter Taylor made a speech and Cloughie made a speech also, talking about courage. They said: 'Courage isn't just tackling and winning the ball. Courage is when Alan goes down the wing and full-backs are sticking the cleats up and he crosses the ball in and doesn't care about getting his leg broken, when they're all trying to get at him. That's courage'." The ribaldry stopped.

Spectators, too, gradually became convinced as Clough and Taylor preached the message and Hinton finally took his place with the Baseball Ground elite. He never did fancy a tackle, but by then, no-one expected it and no-one cared. Hinton was valued in other ways. Perhaps, though, as Taylor shrewdly observed, Hinton was fully appreciated at Derby only after he left.

Hinton had already played three times for England when he was signed from Nottingham Forest in September 1967, but his career had been in decline at the City Ground and he was looking for a move. "I knew a long time before I was signing for Derby County because I remember playing cricket in Nottingham and Peter Taylor came to the cricket game. He and I walked round the cricket field after the game and he told me. 'We're going to sign you for Derby County, but first of all, we have to sign a centre-half and a centre-forward.' And, of course, they went off and signed Roy McFarland, which was an unreal signing, and John O'Hare, and then they came and got me. So I think that was three pretty good signings, but it was what they told me they were going to do. I knew they were ambitious and wanted to do a good job."

Tall and well built for a winger, Hinton played mostly on the left. He belonged there, fitted comfortably. When he went into the middle of the field, he looked out of place, as though he couldn't wait to get back to sanctuary. His ability with both feet was such that it was always a good discussion point, whether he was naturally left, or right-footed. It didn't really matter, 'pinpoint centring' was a phrase which could have been coined for Hinton, either foot. More than anything he proved the adage that talented players respond to those who have faith in them. He made 295 appearances for Derby County, plus 21 as sub, and scored 83 goals.

He has lived for 20 years in America and now works for West Coast television. He is deeply involved with Seattle Sounders, as president, coach and general factotum, and returns to England periodically to bring a team of 'my boys', as he calls them, to play a few matches. When that happens, he visits old friends and entertains them in inimitable style and, just for a while, you think back wistfully and remember Alan Hinton in his pomp – and those splendid white boots.

Jack Howe – a rarity in football

JACK Howe was a rarity in football. He could kick the ball equally well with both feet. Not many players have been able to do that and when taking free-kicks, or corners, they tend to favour one foot – the natural foot – more than the other. Not Howe. "I think one of the best-ever two-footed players was Jack Howe," said Tommy Powell. "I don't know which was his best foot."

Howe joined Derby County from Hartlepools United in March 1936. He made his debut in the penultimate match of that season, against Sunderland, at the Baseball Ground. In those days, the *Derby Evening Telegraph* reporter, who rejoiced under the pseudonym of 'Little Eaton', wrote the following: 'Howe, the Rams new left-back, impressed more by his clean kicking than by his tackling. He made a satisfactory debut and gave promise of forming a valuable partnership with Udall next season.' Pseudonyms were often used by newspapers, which provided anonymity for sports reporters and writers. Perhaps as well. In the following season, Howe and Udall formed a full-back partnership on only seven occasions, although Udall did suffer shoulder trouble.

Derby County beat Sunderland 4-0 on Howe's debut, but the Wearsiders were already League champions. The Rams finished runners-up, eight points behind. The Reserves, though, did win the Central League. It was also the season when Ted Drake scored seven goals for Arsenal against Aston Villa – and also hit the crossbar; 82,905 packed into Stamford Bridge to set a Football League record attendance and saw Chelsea draw with Arsenal; Chesterfield were promoted to Division Two from the Third Division North and Derbyshire won the County Cricket Championship for the first – and only – time in their history. In local sporting terms, 1936 was a very good year.

Jack Howe's big year was yet to come. In the three years before war began, he established himself in the side, at left-back. War service then took him to Scotland, where he 'guested' for several clubs and played for the Scottish League against a British Army XI before being posted abroad. He spent three years in West Africa and India with the Cameroon Highlanders, only arriving back in Britain in time to play in one reserve-team match before being called upon to deputise for Leon Leuty, at centre-half, in the replayed FA Cup semi-final against Birmingham at Maine Road. Intriguingly, it was the very first time he'd played centre-half for Derby County and he only ever played there once again in his career of 244 matches.

Luck then took a further hand. During Howe's absence in the war, Derby-born Jack Parr cemented a place in the team, which in season 1945-46 played in the Football League South. Parr played throughout the Cup run, then broke an arm in a League match against Luton Town, just three weeks before the Cup Final. He joined Sammy Crooks and goalkeeper Frank Boulton on the sidelines at Wembley. Having deputised for Leuty in the semi-final, Howe deputised for Parr in the Final itself. When football returned to normal after the war, Howe reclaimed his place at left back and Parr was squeezed out for long periods. By the time Howe moved on to Huddersfield Town, in 1949, Parr was 29 years old and Derby County were in decline.

There was another twist in tale. In season 1948-49, Howe became the first professional player to wear contact lenses – cost £70 – and shortly afterwards, aged 33, he played for England. That season he won three England caps and also took over the captaincy of Derby County. Jack Howe was certainly an interesting rarity.

Gordon Hughes – enthusiasm and energy

GORDON Hughes played more than 450 matches for three clubs in a professional career that lasted 15 years. Hughes was a traditional right winger with plenty of gusto and a Geordie through and through. He was born in Washington and, like all young lads from that area, his ambition was to play for Newcastle United. In the early 1950s, Newcastle were the FA Cup specialists, winning three Wembley Finals in five years, against Blackpool (1951), Arsenal (1952) and Manchester City (1955). Hughes joined them as a part-time professional from non-League Tow Law Town in 1956 and played 133 League matches and scored 18 goals for the Magpies. Then Tim Ward signed him for Derby County in August 1963.

"I had a bad back injury at Newcastle. I had a spinal fusion and I was out about a year and a half. What they did was they took a bone out of my hip and fused it into the bottom of my spine. I was out a year and a half and while I was out, they signed Dave Hilley. I came back and I was in and out of the side, but I wasn't quite the same player, like. Anyway, Bob Ferguson, who was left full-back for Derby, he's an ex-Newcastle lad, he sort of came up and said 'Why don't you...?', you know. Anyway, I came down and signed on the same day as Alan Durban, at the same table, yes. In the boardroom."

Hughes took over from Don Roby, another dribbling right winger. At that time, Derby County were a free-scoring outfit which also conceded plenty of goals. Hughes's main idea was to get down the outside of the full-back and get the ball across the penalty area. Like all simple ideas, it's one of the best and players like Eddie Thomas, Kevin Hector, Alan Durban and Ian Buxton benefited. Derby County scored 84 goals in season 1964-65 and 71, 68 and 71 in the next three years respectively, but the Rams languished in the middle and lower reaches of the Second Division and Tim Ward was sacked. Then came Brian Clough and Peter Taylor. Hughes played 35 matches under Clough, before he was sold to Lincoln City in March 1968, the same month as Jim Smith joined Lincoln from Halifax Town. Hughes and Smith were teammates at Lincoln and when Smith moved to Boston as player-manager in 1968, Hughes followed him in 1971. The two became firm friends and their friendship has continued ever since.

"I had never any ambition of staying in the game, although I got my full coaching badge. I was an engineer. At Lincoln there was Jim Smith, Graham Taylor, Ray Harford, Mick Brown, who was on the England staff, Billy Taylor, who was also in the England set-up, he died at an early age, but that was five in the Lincoln side who did tremendously well in coaching and managing. Jim was a wing-half, one-paced, but used the ball very well. He was a footballing type and very competitive. He was released by Lincoln when he was 28 years old. He was very upset, as you might imagine, but within a month of being released, he was manager of Boston United and that's were Jim's career started, really."

Hughes played 201 matches for Derby County and scored 24 goals. An easily recognised figure with his small, stocky build, bustling run, receding hairline and flying golden locks in an era when hair was more plentiful, he was a popular player with the fans, who christened him 'Charlie Drake' after the diminutive comedian. They appreciated his enthusiasm and energy. When Hughes went to play at Boston, he reverted to part-time status, living in Derby and working as an engineer at Rolls-Royce. These days he hardly misses a match at Pride Park and an after-the-match chat and 'a bevy' in Jim's office. He has some trenchant views on modern football. Those chats in Jim's office sometimes last a long time

George Jobey – he knew his football

THE first match that Derby County played with George Jobey as manager was away to Hull City on 19 August 1925. The last was at home, against Aston Villa, on 2 September 1939. The following day, war was declared. In between those two dates, Jobey established Derby County as one of the foremost clubs in the country. Derby County were in Division Two when Jobey was appointed manager. Promotion was achieved in his first season and the Rams remained in Division One throughout the rest of his managerial period. Twice they were runners-up, in 1929-30 and 1935-36. Only on three occasions did the Rams finish lower than seventh in the League and during George Jobey's 13 seasons at Derby County, seventh was the overall average position in Division One. Although Jobey never won a major trophy, it could be argued it was the most sustained, successful period in Derby County's history.

Jobey was born at Heddon-on-Tyne, just outside Newcastle, in 1885. He played for Morpeth Harriers before joining Newcastle United when he was 21 years old. He never established himself in the first team, although he played ten times in Newcastle's championship team of 1908-09. Curiously, Newcastle lost 9-1 at home to Sunderland and 6-5 to Liverpool at Anfield in 1909-10, but still won the League by seven points. Jobey did win an FA Cup medal in 1911, albeit a loser's one, when Bradford City, fielding eight Scotsmen, beat the Magpies 1-0 in a replay at Old Trafford, after drawing 0-0 at the Crystal Palace. In 1913, Jobey joined Woolwich Arsenal and scored the first goal for the Gunners at their new Highbury home. He than damaged ankle ligaments and was wheeled home on a milk cart by a supporter who was a dairyman in Gillespie Road. In that match he played at centre-forward, but he was really an industrious half-back. Then came the war. After the war, he joined Leicester City and later played for Northampton Town before joining Wolverhampton Wanderers, in 1922, as manager-coach. Wolves were immediately relegated to the Third Division, but Jobey won promotion the following season and it was a major surprise when he resigned 1924, to become an hotelier. He ran an hotel for a year, before being persuaded to join Derby County.

Jobey's style of management was based on fear. He was a rigid disciplinarian and few players were not in awe of him. He seldom attended training sessions and, when he did, it was usually to order haircuts all round. His skill was in his judgment of players and how they would blend together in a team. Thirteen of the players that Jobey signed went on to become international players, 11 of them at Derby County, a tribute to his keen eye for talent. He signed 83 players during his time at the club, including eight internationals, plus most of the team that won the FA Cup in 1946. A total of 79 players departed in that time. Perhaps his most notable 'name' signings were Harry Bedford and Hughie Gallagher, and his ability in the transfer market was legendary. Alf Jeffries played under Jobey: "I'll tell you one thing. They used to say all kinds of things about him, but he knew his football did Jobey and he knew the players, oh aye. He used to drink port wine and could get a bit tipsy. He smoked corona cigars, too."

In August 1941, a joint FA and Football League commission sat at Derby to investigate allegations of irregularities at Derby County between 1925 and 1938. The outcome was that George Jobey was permanently suspended. Four directors – Alderman H. G. Pattison, Bendle-Moore, H. T. Ann and Ben Robshaw – were suspended *sine die* as was a former director O. J. Jackson. Former director A. Green was suspended for three years. Secretary W. S. Moore was severely censured and the club was fined £500. 'Financial irregularities' was the charge; bonuses and 'under-the-counter' payments had been made, contrary to the rules; false accounts had been kept. How Jobey had attracted such eminent players to the Baseball Ground became clear, but it should not detract from his ability as a manager. The pieces had to fit together and, for most of the time, they did. After the war, Jobey's suspension was lifted but it wasn't until 1952 that he returned to the game, as manager of Mansfield Town, remarkably to be sacked soon afterwards for 'lack of interest'.

In 1962, in Bangor Street, Chaddesden, George Jobey, the arch wheeler-dealer, who ruled his players with a rod of iron, died.

Errington Keen – a step too far?

ERRINGTON 'Ike' Keen joined Derby County from Newcastle United in 1930, just before Christmas. His one match for Newcastle United was against the Rams and manager George Jobey signed the flaxen-haired wing-half a couple of months later. Keen went on to play 237 times for Derby County, won four England caps and played for the Football League against Scottish League in 1936-37. He was a member of the team that finished runners-up in the old Division One in 1935-36. The Derby County half-back line of Nicholas, Barker, Keen appeared together no fewer than 180 times, once they got together against West Bromwich Albion in October 1931. That match was lost 4-0, but the trio must have done something right because they survived for the next match. In fact manager George Jobey only made one change and the Rams responded by beating Birmingham 3-1 at the Baseball Ground.

If Nicholas was a tough, but rather crude player on the right, Keen was the opposite on the left. He was an artistic type in what would now be called an attacking midfield role, but like all players of his style he was criticised at times for his lack of defensive discipline. With centre-half Jack Barker also inclined to attack, Derby County became the 'nearly' team of the 1930s. Arsenal adopted a policy of using their best players in the FA Cup, but, because of injuries, resting them for League matches. Rotation? The Football League was not impressed and fined Arsenal £250 for fielding below-strength teams. The League also rejected the idea of having two referees controlling a match, despite successful experiments in amateur football. Times change, but sometimes not as much as some people think.

Keen first played for Derby County at right-half, as deputy for Johnny McIntyre, but he soon moved to the opposite flank and made the left-half position his own. He was to remain there until he lost his place to the emerging Tim Ward in the middle of season 1937-38. He was not retained at the end of that season and joined non-League Chelmsford City. Keen had made three appearances for England in the previous season, which meant his demise was rapid. It denoted two things. One was that Jobey was not adverse to changing his personnel rapidly. The second was that it didn't matter how eminent a player was, he was only on a one-year contract. This meant that the flow of players was much easier to facilitate than in the modern era of long contracts. The financial implications, as far as clubs were concerned, were much less and clubs were able to carry very large professional staffs. As far as players were concerned, competition for places was fierce and there was always the retained list, or otherwise, around the corner.

There might have been another factor in the particular case of Ike Keen. Clubs then were able, at their discretion, to pay a benefit to a players who had completed five years' service. There was a fixed maximum amount and Keen received a benefit cheque of £650 in March 1936. Keen invested the money in a business which failed and he finished up in Derby Bankruptcy Court. Alf Jeffries remembers: "He'd opened up a tea business called 'Rington's' or 'Errington's', or something like that. Errington was his first name, of course. He was a gambler and liked to go to the dogs at Derby, Long Eaton and Nottingham and places like that. Sammy [Crooks] liked to go to the dogs as well. Anyway, Ike used to put his hand in the till. Of course, if he won, he never put it back and Jobey rescued him twice from the tax man. You talk as you find and I always found Jobey very good." Perhaps Ike Keen had taken a step to far, even for Jobey.

Francis Lee – supremely confident

FRANCIS Lee will always be associated with Manchester City, like Charlie George is with Arsenal. Both played for Derby County, with great success, but the roots are too deep to think of them as 'proper' Derby County players. Not, for example, like Kevin Hector and Colin Todd. Hector and Todd each played more than 150 League games for Bradford Park Avenue and Sunderland respectively, but the main emphasis of their careers was with Derby County.

Despite that, some of Francis Lee's performances for the Rams were outstanding and one was truly memorable. That was his dust-up with Norman Hunter at the Baseball Ground in November 1975. These days Hunter is rather sheepish about the whole thing. What Lee's feelings about it are I have no idea, but Charlie George had it about right when he observed: "I think there'd been a bit of niggle about a penalty incident earlier. Anyway, they certainly had a go. It's hard to imagine what would have happened these days. It was a good contest." It was, indeed. No-one could ever accuse Lee of doing things by halves.

Lee began his career at Bolton Wanderers. He played in Division One as a 16-year-old – in the same side as Nat Lofthouse – and even then was branching out with some business interests. He played 189 League games for Bolton and scored 92 goals, which for someone who played many of those games on the right wing is a healthy ratio. He was transferred to Manchester City in 1967 and became one of the fabled three – Mike Summerbee, Colin Bell and Lee – around which much Sky Blue folklore has been woven. City won the championship, the FA Cup, the League Cup and the European Cup-winners' Cup under the astute managerial partnership of Joe Mercer and Malcolm Allison and played some wonderfully attractive football. Lee won 27 caps and was a member of the World Cup squad which unsuccessfully attempted to retain the Jules Rimet Trophy, in the heat and humidity of Mexico, in 1970.

Dave Mackay paid £100,000 for Lee at the start of the 1974-75 season. He wore the number 11 shirt, but played as a support striker, with Kevin Hector, alongside centre-forward Roger Davies. He scored 12 goals in 34 appearances, including a spectacular effort at Maine Road against his former club, which had Barry Davies, on *Match of the Day*, reaching for the superlatives. By the end of the season, Lee had another championship medal, this time with Derby County.

Lee was a supremely confident player, all bustle and barrel chest, like a peacock in a hurry, and he was always noticeable on the pitch. He could also show the continentals a thing or two about how to win a penalty, but he was the sort of player whose temperament meant he lived on the edge of trouble. His absence, through suspension, for the second leg of the European Cup-tie against Real Madrid, after the Rams won the first leg at the Baseball Ground 4-1, cost Derby County dear. Derby lost 5-1 after extra-time in the Bernabeau Stadium and with Bruce Rioch out through injury and Roy McFarland and Henry Newton able to play only after receiving pain-killing injections, Lee's absence was keenly felt.

Lee played ended his playing career at Derby County in characteristic style. The final match of the 1975-76 season, at Ipswich, was to be his 500th and last League appearance (499, plus one as substitute). The Rams won 6-2, Lee scored twice. It could hardly have been better stage managed. He scored a total of 229 League goals, 24 for Derby County in 62 League appearances. He signed-off like the true showman he is and then went off to train racehorses and become, for a while, chairman and virtual owner of Manchester City.

Jack Lee – another England striker

MANY Derby County supporters remember that Francis Lee played centre-forward for Derby County and for England. Not too many people are aware that 25 years earlier, another Lee did likewise. He was Jack Lee, no relation to Francis and, in physical build and style, a totally different type of player.

Jack Lee was tall and angular and injury stalked his career, which began at Leicester City in 1946. He played 123 League matches for Leicester and scored 74 goals. He also played in the Leicester City team beaten 3-1 by Wolverhampton Wanderers in the 1949 FA Cup Final. Leicester were in the Second Division at the time and were no match for the Wolves, particularly because they were without Don Revie, because of a nose injury received in the semi-final. In a controversial selection, Lee moved to inside-right for the Final, to accommodate reserve full-back Jim Harrison at centre-forward. Harrison scored only one goal in his career at Leicester. For Wolves, it was manager Stan Cullis's first trophy and his team went on to dominate the 1950s, with three League championships, three runners-up positions and two FA Cup successes. Two of the 1949 Cup Final goals came from Jesse Pye, later to become a Rams favourite.

Lee was top scorer at Leicester in the following season, with 22 goals, and so it was a shock to Leicester supporters when he was transferred to Derby County for £12,500 in the close season of 1950. Jack Stamps moved to inside-right to accommodate the newcomer, who soon became a success. Derby lost the first two matches of the new season, without Lee scoring, but he made up for that in the next six games by scoring nine goals. His scoring burst earned him his only England cap, against Northern Ireland in a 4-1 victory. Lee scored, but he was dropped for the next game, in favour of Jackie Milburn. After having fielded internationals galore in the 1930s and early post-war years, it was almost another 21 years before Roy McFarland was selected to play for England against Malta in a European qualifying tie in 1971 to become the next Derby County player to be capped.

Lee went on to score 28 League goals that season and missed only three games, one of which was the last match of the season against Charlton Athletic at The Valley, because he'd received a knee injury in the previous match against Everton. He had suffered with cartilage trouble whilst at Leicester and the latest injury required an operation and then another. Lee was never as effective again, despite making 27 League appearances and scoring 16 goals in the 1952-53 season. It couldn't save Derby County from relegation from Division One. In Division Two, Lee scored six times in 19 League games as Jack Barker took over from Stuart McMillan and Derby County continued to slide. He didn't appear in the first team again after the end of March and left for Coventry City in November 1954, retiring from football at the end of that season. Despite his injury problems, Lee scored 56 goals in 99 appearances for the Rams. An old-fashioned, bustling type of player, perhaps he didn't quite have the strength of physique to cope with the rigours of the centre-forward's job in an age when part of the centre-half's job was to let the centre-forward know he'd been in a contest. The Baseball Ground mud probably didn't help, either.

Jack Lee had another claim to fame. He played as an amateur for Leicestershire at cricket in 1947. A medium-pace bowler, he took a wicket with the first ball he bowled in county cricket, against Glamorgan. It was the only wicket he ever took, in the only match he ever played. One cap for England, one wicket for Leicestershire. A unique 'double.'

Leon Leuty – the best of all?

HOW good was Leon Leuty? In the pantheon of great Derby County centre-halves – Barker, McFarland, Wright, Stimac, perhaps Carbonari – where did Leuty rate? Some say the best of all. Ray Young: "I didn't see Jack Barker play. I saw Leon Leuty play. Leon was there when I signed for Derby. Stylish, but hard as well. Oh yes, he was hard. Only about my height, about 5ft 10ins. Oh yes, a good player. I think he was the best centre-half I've seen at Derby." Don Hazledine: "Leon Leuty I would pick out as the best, but I did like McFarland's play. I think he was a tremendous player as well. Lovely style, Leuty. Cultured." Supporter Bill Brownson saw them all: "Jack Barker was great, but the best centre-half in my time was Leon Leuty, without a doubt. Very stylish. Leuty was unfortunate because he came up when Neil Franklin of Stoke was at his best. That was unfortunate because it kept him out of the England team. I think if Leuty had got into the England team, he would have stayed there." In fact Leuty captained England 'B' whilst at Derby and played in the unofficial full international in aid of the Bolton Disaster Fund. He also played twice for the Football League.

Leon Leuty first signed for Derby County as an amateur in 1936 but during World War Two he guested for Notts County when he was working at Rolls-Royce. He was also a member of the fine Derby Corinthians team which included players like Tommy Powell and Reg Harrison. In August 1943 the Rams re-signed Leuty as an amateur and then as a professional in May 1944. He was one of the players who won an FA Cup winners' medal before he had played a proper League game, at centre-half in the famous 1946 Wembley win over Charlton. One of a fine Derby team of the late 1940s, he was one of several players who became unsettled after the Rams signed Billy Steel. In March 1950, after 158 League and Cup games for Derby, he went to Bradford Park Avenue for £20,000. Six months later, Notts County paid £25,000 for his signature.

I saw Leuty play, once. The occasion sticks in the memory for various reasons, Sheffield Wednesday v Notts County at Hillsborough. Most of our family were Wednesdayites and my father and I used to stand on the Leppings Lane End terraces. In 1951, our hero was centre-forward Derek Dooley. Red hair, raw-boned, a goalscorer. 'Six foot two, eyes of blue, our Dooley, Dooley fair,' we used to sing, to the Guy Mitchell hit number *Truly, Truly Fair*. The crowd loved him.

It was a wet day and the spray was flying. Wednesday kicked towards our goal in the first half and, although it was 1-0 at half-time, Dooley wasn't getting much change out of Leuty, who we were told was one of the best centre-halves in England. We knew the famous Tommy Lawton would be in our penalty area after the interval. He wasn't there much. Wednesday scored five goals in the second half – and Dooley scored all five! Leuty didn't know which way to go and Dooley chested in the final goal in front of a sea of blue and white. Unfortunately for us, those goals were at the Spion Kop end, so we only saw them in the distance, through the rain.

Two years later, Dooley collided with the Preston North End goalkeeper, George Thompson, at Deepdale and broke his leg. Gangerine set in; the leg was amputated. It was February 1953. Dooley had scored 62 goals in 61 League games and he was just 23 years old. That was tragic enough, but a greater tragedy was to come. Less than two years later, Leon Leuty, aged 35, died. He was a victim of leukaemia.

Martin McDonnell – enjoyed a sliding tackle

WHEN he took over as manager of Derby County in July 1955, Harry Storer made two immediate signings, in his view both vital if he was to steer the Rams out of the uncompromising surroundings of the Third Division North. One was a footballer, through and through, the skilful Irish international midfielder and inspirational captain, Reg Ryan. The other was Martin McDonnell.

Storer liked his defenders to defend and it was the third time he had signed McDonnell, a former paratrooper and a man whose Derby County legend was to become established in the rough and tumble of Northern Section football. McDonnell was born in Newton-le-Willows, Lancashire, in 1924 and during World War Two he played for Everton, making his debut at centre-half against Bury at Gigg Lane in a League North game. He was in and out of the Everton side in those wartime years of guest players and whoever was available, but he did play with Tommy Lawton. Martin McDonnell and Tommy Lawton in the same side – not a lot of people know that.

By August 1946, the dawn of the first post-war League season, McDonnell had moved to Southport, who that campaign struggled to avoid having to seek re-election to the Third Division North. McDonnell played 38 times.

At the end of that season Harry Storer, then managing Birmingham City, signed McDonnell for the first time, and playing in front of Gil Merrick, later to become one of England's best-known goalkeepers, McDonnell helped Birmingham to the Second Division championship in his first season at St Andrew's. His appearances in the top flight were strictly limited, although interestingly one was at centre-forward in a 1-0 home defeat by Derby when he was in direct opposition to none other than Leon Leuty.

In November that season Storer returned to manage Coventry City, where he had been in charge from 1931 to 1945. McDonnell, meanwhile, had failed to mpress new Birmingham manager Bob Brocklebank and in October 1949 Storer signed McDonnell again. Coventry were mid-table in Division Two and McDonnell went straight into the side at right-back and missed only two games for the rest of the season, ending the campaign back at centre-half. In 1950-51 he was ever-present and stayed in the side right through relegation to the Third Division South. Storer resigned in November 1953 but when he returned to football 20 months later with the Rams, Martin McDonnell was one of his first signings; he had made 245 League and Cup appearances for City and had massive experience of fighting it out in the Third Division.

McDonnell was a hard man, but most of all, enjoyed a sliding tackle. Spectators in the Baseball Ground paddock in front of the main stand would sway backwards and cringe as McDonnell launched himself towards them on a wet day, spray flying – and forwards too! Then there was his forward roll, executed after a tackle and probably a legacy of his days as a paratrooper.

In 1955-56, Derby finished runners-up to Grimsby Town – only one side went up from each Third Division section in those days – and McDonnell played in the first half of the season before losing his place to Ken Oliver. He got back in the side at Wrexham a few games into 1956-57 and stayed there as Derby won the title in swashbuckling style. As the Rams settled back into Division Two, McDonnell missed only ten games, but the Derby team had too many old legs and in July 1958 he went back into the Third Division North to sign for perennial strugglers Crewe Alexandra. After 17 games for the Alex – for whom he apparently played for several weeks before noticing that he had suffered a broken toe – McDonnell's League career was over, after 412 appearances for five clubs. He never managed to score a goal.

Martin McDonnell died in Coventry in April 1988.

Roy McFarland – good enough for any team

ROY McFarland may not have been the best player the Rams ever had, nor the best player who ever played for the Rams, but McFarland was the best player I've seen play for Derby County. Some say that McFarland could have played in any position on the field. I don't think so. Brian Clough tried him in midfield. The experiment was abandoned after one match. In any case, there was no need to play McFarland anywhere else than at centre-half. His influence from the position was immense. To watch him play was like watching a thoroughbred racehorse in action. McFarland had football class. Whatever class is, McFarland had it. He had critics. He wasn't the quickest, although he could hold his own before injuries caught up with him; his right foot was a swinger; he didn't do tricks on the ball; some felt he wasn't tall enough to be really dominant in the air, but I didn't see him lose many. All such perceived deficiencies may be true to some extent, but in the end, it all comes back to Harry Storer's deceptively simple criteria: "Can he play?" Professionals understand. The answer is "Yes." Some good judges even felt that McFarland was good enough to play in any team in the world in the early 1970s.

He was one of Brian Clough's most bizarre signings. McFarland was playing for Tranmere Rovers when Clough and Taylor came knocking on his father's door in August 1967. It was McFarland's father that Clough targeted. Said McFarland, "They worked on my Dad and, without doubt, found the weak link with my father. They chatted to him, talked about the old days, talked about the old players. My Dad, in a sense, was mesmerised, he loved talking football, loved football himself and at the end, I turned round to my father and said I would like it left to the following morning."

Clough takes up the tale. "So, he comes down in his striped pyjamas, I'm rabbiting on to him and they'd got the biggest log fire you'd ever seen in your life. And his Dad said, 'You sit here Brian.' So I'm in front of this bloody fire and the sweat is running down my back. I'm sitting there and the missus is giving me cups of tea that I didn't want, but you know what swung it? I'll swear to you – his Dad said [to Roy McFarland], 'I want a word with you.' Went into the back kitchen, didn't close the door. I'm earwigging and he said, 'You sign for Brian.' He signed."

McFarland stands third on Derby County's all-time appearances list behind Kevin Hector and Ron Webster, with 525 appearances plus five as substitute. He is seventh in League appearances with 437, plus five as substitute. He played 28 times for England between 1971 and 1976 and it was at Wembley, playing for England, where he suffered a ruptured achilles tendon that kept him out of all but the last four matches of Derby County's second championship season in 1974-75. In his career he also scored 48 goals. For someone who didn't take penalties, or played in attack on occasions, that is a considerable number.

He became player-manager of Bradford City in 1981 and led them to promotion from Division Four, a feat he was later to repeat with Cambridge United in 1998-99 (although by then they called it Division Three). He returned from Bradford to become assistant to Peter Taylor – an acrimonious 'transfer' with allegations flowing back and forth and a secretly-recorded boardroom conversation – and played a few matches in 1983-84. When Arthur Cox became manager in 1984, McFarland became his assistant and when Cox left Derby in 1993, McFarland took over as manager. He wasn't able to achieve the promotion to the top flight that the directors and fans craved and in the 1994-95 season, 33 players were used, a club record. He left at the end of that season, having spent 27 of the previous 28 years with Derby County. Ironically, Liverpool was the club he always hoped to play for. Said McFarland: "It never happened and, without doubt, if I look back on my career there's no regrets that I never played for Liverpool Football Club, because signing for Derby County was the best thing that ever happened to me." He's lived in Derby since the day he signed, although he now manages Torquay United.

Was he the best? "McFarland was, for me, the best player. No question, overall. You had your Todds, and Gemmills, Hennessey and O'Hare, Hector, the whole lot of 'em, but to me, McFarland was the best player, no question." Would you argue with Dave Mackay?

John McGovern – a knitter-together

WHEN a gawky 19-year-old right winger with a jerky running action turned up at the Baseball Ground in September 1968, many people thought that manager Brian Clough had taken leave of his senses in paying a fee of £7,500 to Hartlepools United. McGovern had few obvious footballing assets. He had no pace, no dribbling ability, didn't score many goals, wasn't good in the air, had a very moderate left foot, didn't particularly frighten anyone with the power of his tackling. The terrace devotees were not impressed. They were not slow to show their displeasure either and McGovern was subjected to some severe abuse in his early days with Derby County.

Now McGovern can afford to smile. Few players have managed to win the honours he has done in the game. Not many players have captained a team to successive European Cup wins, as he did with Nottingham Forest in 1979 and 1980. He won League championship medals with two clubs, Derby County in 1972 and Nottingham Forest in 1978. He won two League Cup winners' medals in successive years with Nottingham Forest and might have won a third in a row had Peter Shilton and David Needham not got in a tangle and allowed Andy Gray to score an easy winner for Wolverhampton Wanderers in 1980. Promotion campaigns, Charity Shield appearances, World Club Championship matches, McGovern experienced them all. He played 523 League matches for five clubs in a professional career that lasted 19 years. As Joe Mercer once finally said, in exasperation, when a pipsqueak newspaper reporter persistently questioned his judgment in a football matter: "Okay then, show us your medals."

What McGovern could do was make it easy for others. He was a 'knitter-together' of bits and pieces. His positional play was excellent, particularly when he moved from the wider right position he was allocated at Derby, to a more central role at Forest. His ball control was very good indeed and that compensated for other deficiencies in his game. He was well aware of those. Few players knew their own game better than McGovern. His shrewd football intelligence was allied to a discipline to stick to the things he could do. McGovern may not have had outstanding talent, but he had loads of ability, which is a completely different and more important asset. What he also had was the good fortune to catch the eye of a management duo like Brian Clough and Peter Taylor, who were prepared to back their judgment with the gawky youth from Montrose. They saw McGovern's potential when many others were not impressed. Perhaps, too, Clough was a father figure for the young Scotsman, whose own father died when he was 11 years old. Said McGovern: "I thrived on discipline and never had any hesitation in signing for him." He did too, four times in total, at Hartlepools, Derby County, Leeds United and Nottingham Forest. It did McGovern no harm at all, although he took a drop in wages to rejoin Clough at Forest, after the abortive experience at Leeds. "Show us your medals," goes the football saying – and McGovern, eventually, did.

Paul McGrath – life in the old dog

I NEVER realised how good a player Paul McGrath was until he joined Derby County. Ron Atkinson once labelled him the 'best defender in Europe', but Big Ron has sometimes been known to go slightly over the top and, after all, McGrath had played under Atkinson at Old Trafford. Whatever the testimonials, it's always best to make up your own mind on these things, if you get the chance.

The chance came when Jim Smith signed the big Irishman with the dodgy knees, in September 1996. It was Derby County's first season in the Premiership and experience was important. How had Smith persuaded McGrath to the Baseball Ground? "He didn't have to say a lot really," said McGrath. "I've met him before, through Ron, and I've the utmost respect for him. I mean, we sat down for a quarter of an hour, or so and I was wanting to sign. He's got that sort of magnetism really. There's a few managers that do have, that make players want to play for them and it was very, very simple."

McGrath played one season for Derby County before he left for a very brief period at Sheffield United. He played 23 matches in the Premiership, plus one as substitute, and in many of them gave a master-class in the central defender's art. His reading of the game was outstanding and, despite being 37 years old, he retained enough sharpness off the mark and quickness over ten yards, to show younger opponents that there was life in the old dog yet. In between offering glimpses of what a powerful and formidable player he must have been at his peak, he also gave the impression of enjoying the game. Clearly he took football itself very seriously, but he appeared not to take himself too seriously in it. That attitude conveyed itself to supporters and, as a consequence, they loved him on the Popside. "Paul McGrath – he limps on water," they used to sing and McGrath would grin, a little sheepishly.

When he played with Igor Stimac, usually in a back-three system, there were echoes of the quality of the Roy McFarland and Colin Todd era, particularly in the way they distribution of the ball from the back, with composure and confidence. There is no doubt that he brought a different dimension to the team's defensive play in that critical first season in the Premiership.

McGrath made his debut for Manchester United in 1982 and had some interesting views on how football had changed during his career: "There are more athletes. I think back to when I started, there were probably more footballers, really good footballers, you know, lads on the ball and that stuff. Now there's a lot of speed merchants in the game. That's why there's a lot of shirt holding." He thought Mark Hughes, Alan Shearer and Ian Wright were difficult opponents, but the centre-forward who gave him most trouble was none of those. "Kerry Dixon was a player I found difficult to handle. He had great spring. That used to be my strength, heading the ball. He used to annoy me when he beat me, but he was quick on the deck as well. I know people are surprised when I say that, but he was one of the toughest opponents I ever had."

He didn't train much at Derby. He wasn't a believer in leaving energy on the training ground, but his knees weren't a problem. "No, really. I've no complaints about my knees. I'm thrilled that I've lasted this long. I've been blessed, I think, that I'm able to sit around all week and then, on Saturday, try and play, so... I'm really lucky." Those who saw him play were lucky, too. Paul McGrath, he was as confident and smooth as 'the Murphy's'.

Johnny McIntyre – a love of football

I FIRST met Johnny McIntyre in Harry Storer's rather dark and dingy office. As was usually the case, Storer's dog, Bill, lay at the bottom of the three steps which led down into the room, which had a bar on one side, and Johnny 'Mac' sort of lurked around the edges of the place. He was a smallish chap with a serious-looking face, but while I was conscious of his presence, I couldn't really understand what he was supposed to be doing. Then it became apparent. Storer took a coin out of his pocket – a half-crown, I think – and flicked it into the air. Johnny 'Mac' caught it in a well-practised way and disappeared. No word passed between them. Five minutes later he was back, apparently from the corner shop, with a packet of 20 cigarettes.

Johnny 'Mac' was one of those valuable people at football clubs who keeps things ticking over. He was for some years the right-hand man to chief scout Charlie Elliott and he kept an eye on the 'A' team performances, amongst other things. People at the club knew that he had been a Rams player in days gone by, but as those days were the 1920s, there were few who had actually seen him play. As is the custom though, in professional sport, accumulated knowledge and wisdom is passed on through the generations and it was commonly accepted that Johnny 'Mac' must have been a pretty good player to have played 369 games for Derby County – it puts him 11th on Derby County's all-time League list – alongside some of the greatest names of the past. As a consequence, when you came across him, usually wearing a crumpled tweed jacket and walking a bit stiffly along one of the corridors under 'B' Stand at the Baseball Ground, his pieces of advice and words of encouragement were valued and well respected, especially by the younger players. Most of all, his love of football shone through in his muttered conversations, which meant that in a way, Johnny 'Mac' seemed ageless. It was quite a shock when he left the club, in 1961. His service, on and off the field to Derby County, filled almost 30 years.

He joined Derby County in 1921, from Stenhousemuir, as an inside-forward and scored on his debut against Blackpool, but he settled into the side at right-half as an industrious midfield type of player. Short in stature, he was sometimes described as 'stout' in journals of the day, but despite being dogged by injuries at various times, he held his place, being captain when Derby County finished runners-up in Division One in 1929-30. He was transferred to Chesterfield in 1931, but two years later he retired from full-time football to return to Derby to become a licensee. He was dismayed to find that it prevented him playing local league football on Saturdays, so his solution was to turn out for Derby Co-op in the Derby and District Wednesday League.

Dave Mackay – already a legend

WHEN Dave Mackay signed for Derby County, few people actually believed it had happened. Mackay was a legend before he came to Derby, but he wasn't finished yet. Supporters who were lucky enough to see him play for the Rams could only marvel at the player he must have been in his prime, for when Dave Mackay came to Derby County, aged 33, he was older than his manager! Brian Clough maintains that Mackay was one of his three best-ever signings.

There was an aura about Mackay. Television images linger. Of him almost throttling Billy Bremner, by holding him by the front of his shirt with one hand, like a sack of potatoes, so that the fiery Leeds captain was forced to stand on tip-toe. Hoisting aloft the FA Cup, for Tottenham at Wembley in 1967 after making a comeback from twice breaking his leg. Seeing him live in matches, almost casually sending the ball unerringly on its way, left-footed, with such a beautiful flowing action. "Don't move," he'd shout, in training. "I'll plonk it." Most of all, was the dynamic picture of him leading Derby County out on to the pitch, before every match. Not for him the dawdle; not for him the slow jog. When Mackay led Derby County out on to the Baseball Ground pitch, he came out of the tunnel like the engine on the front of an express train, smoke belching, steam flying, whistle blowing – and the team close behind. The message was abundantly clear: 'Anyone getting in the way today, is going to suffer'.

At Tottenham, Mackay was a dynamo in midfield, but for Derby County he played at the back. "Easy," he says, characteristically. So easy, in fact, that he was joint Footballer of the Year when Derby County were promoted as champions of the old Second Division, in 1969. Next season, they finished fourth in Division One, with an average attendance of 35,924 packing the Baseball Ground. The following season, for the first time in his career, Mackay played every one of the 42 League games. Then, suddenly, he was gone. To Swindon Town, as player-manager. He moved on to Nottingham Forest and then, after the fiasco of the Clough-Taylor resignation in 1973, he returned to the Baseball Ground as manager.

He led the Rams to the championship again, in 1975. The following season they finished fourth. They also lost, controversially, in the semi-final of the FA Cup, to Manchester United. A poor start to season 1975-76 led to Mackay asking the board for a vote of confidence. He didn't get it. As he puts it: "Dave Mackay sacked himself." It was November 1976. Once again, most people couldn't believe it.

Supporter Brian Flint sums up the Mackay phenomenon: "My biggest buzz – and I still get hairs at the back of my neck prickling – was when I was delivering night papers... and the headline said, 'Rams sign Dave Mackay.' If I see him today, I still get those prickles. Nobody else, nobody else, just him... well, he was a legend, wasn't he? After that [signing], very good players came, but not the same. The impact wasn't the same. He was Dave Mackay."

Stuart McMillan – Cup Final manager

STUART McMillan had quite a remarkable career. He was one of only ten players in the 20th century who played both county cricket for Derbyshire and professional football for Derby County, but he went one better. Like Harry Storer, he managed Derby County as well. Furthermore, he led them to victory in the 1946 FA Cup Final. Yet he was limited as a player and as a manager. If being in the right place at the right time is an essential part of professional sporting success, Stuart McMillan was living proof.

He actually played just one match for Derbyshire at cricket and four matches for Derby County at football. During the war, he acted as a scout and an 'advisor' to the club, whilst running the Nag's Head in Mickleover. Some of his duties included driving officials, including directors, to matches. That must have worked in his favour because when Ted Magner left Derby County to work abroad, in January 1946, McMillan took over as manager. Derby County were already in the fourth round of the FA Cup and so McMillan inherited the Cup-winning team. After the war he twice broke the British transfer record with purchases of Billy Steel and Johnny Morris. In 1947-48 Derby County finished fourth in Division One and reached the FA Cup semi-final where they lost to a Manchester United team that contained Morris, later to sign for Derby County. The following year they finished third in the table, but as the 1940s gave way to the 1950s, the club was sliding and McMillan was replaced, in 1953, by Jack Barker, who couldn't halt the descent into the Third Division North.

McMillan's father, Johnny, had also played for Derby County in the days of Steve Bloomer. He was an outside-right who scored 50 goals in 126 matches for the Rams between 1891 and 1896. Later, McMillan senior managed Gillingham, who were members of the Southern League, and he signed Stuart after the latter had been at Chelsea without making a first-team appearance. Nepotism? Perhaps. Stuart McMillan played 30 matches for Gillingham before leaving for Wolverhampton Wanderers, shortly before his father got the sack. Gillingham had by that time accumulated huge debts. McMillan played 22 times at Molineux, but in 1922-23 Wolves were relegated to the Third Division North for the first time in their history. He played 14 times when they were promoted the following season and then left to join Bradford City. He made 73 appearances at Valley Parade and then joined Nottingham Forest, making only seven appearances, before joining Clapton Orient. He ended his playing days at Orient after 24 matches. He then followed his father into the licensed trade in Derby, where he was well known for liking a drink, or two. Then, he became manager of Derby County.

"He had a twitch in his nose," said Ray Young. "Somebody said it was a whisky twitch because he drank a bottle of whisky a day. It used to move. Most of the time when I was in his office I couldn't take my eyes off the nose twitching." Said Reg Harrison: "He was a gentleman, but he wasn't a good manager. He didn't come in and take charge. He wasn't 'the boss', if you follow me." McMillan was good enough at golf to represent Derbyshire and golf was one of Johnny Morris's abiding pleasures. Still is. Morris has a forthright view of McMillan's capabilities: "Stuart, as I've said before, was the best manager I've played for – until he started talking about football!" Maybe, but Stuart McMillan was Derby County's manager when the Rams won the Cup and there hasn't been another.

Ted McMinn – the Tin Man

'TED' McMinn's real name is Kevin, although 'Unpredictable' might be in there somewhere. Jimmy Greaves christened him 'The Tin Man' when he was playing for Glasgow Rangers. Throughout his career, managers, coaches, colleagues and supporters probably had some well-chosen names for him as well. Often referred to as 'a character' – which covers a wide spectrum – McMinn was good enough to be chosen by supporters in a poll, to play outside-right in an all-time Derby County XI.

Tall, bony and gangly, he wasn't the archetypal winger in build. He was, though, a Scottish dribbler, who, when things went well, could destroy defences with apparent ease. On such days at the Baseball Ground the crowd seemed to sway with him as he embarked on a mazy run, and a buzz of anticipation went round the ground whenever he received the ball. Usually it was with his right foot, on the left wing, in front of the Pop-siders. When it was not his day, he was infuriating to watch and, most likely, annoying to be playing with. Like it or not, it was impossible to ignore McMinn and there was no doubting his popularity, which was probably as much a tribute to his obvious enthusiasm for playing the game as to his actual performance on any given day.

McMinn's career was unusual before he came to Derby County. He joined Glasgow Rangers from Queen of the South in 1984. At Ibrox Park he produced some flamboyant performances which put him into consideration for international honours, but it didn't materialise and in 1987 he left Rangers to play, surprisingly, for Seville in Spain. Not too many British players had played abroad at that time, but there was a reason for McMinn moving to the sunshine. It was that the manager of Seville was the formidable Jock Wallace. He had been McMinn's manager at Rangers and had himself moved to Seville. It's hard to imagine what the Spaniards made of Wallace. His Scots brogue was thick enough for even the Scots to have difficulty understanding him at times. Unfortunately for McMinn, Wallace left Seville six months after McMinn arrived, so within another six months, McMinn was back in England, signed by Arthur Cox for Derby County.

McMinn found the experience in Spain valuable and he learned much, for despite his apparently casual style of play, McMinn is a serious student of football. He also has a good reputation as a coach, in which capacity he was assistant manager at Conference side Southport and is now assistant to Mark Wright at Oxford United. It sounds a little bit like 'poacher turned gamekeeper', for McMinn readily admits that he used to give Cox nightmares with occasional lapses of discipline, on the pitch.

What McMinn didn't lack was courage. The horrendous knee ligament injury he suffered playing against Tottenham Hotspur at White Hart Lane kept him out of action for more than a year, but he returned to become Derby's Player of the Year in 1991-92. It's an honour he values with much pride. Despite other serious injuries, which curtailed their appearances together, McMinn and Gary Micklewhite formed a well-balanced wing pairing which provided ammunition at various times for strikers like Dean Saunders, Paul Goddard and Mick Harford.

He left Derby County for Birmingham City in the close season of 1993 and later moved to Burnley, before the knees began to ache and he retired. He returned to Derby to coach in the junior academy before receiving the call from his former colleague and great friend Mark Wright at Southport. It's safe to say that Ted McMinn is one of Derby County's favourite sons.

Reg Matthews – what a repertoire!

MODERN players are sometimes referred to as athletes. Reg Matthews was a gymnast. Cats have the ability to twist themselves so that the front end can face upwards while the back end faces downwards. Could Reg Matthews do that? It certainly looked like it sometimes and in an age when telescopic lenses were rare and photographers sat on their bags on the by-line alongside the goals, hoping for goalmouth action, Matthews provided them with a host of spectacular photographs some of which defied belief. Like the high-flying trapeze artists in the big-top circuses, Matthews could draw involuntary 'oohs' and 'aaahs' from crowds up and down the land, as he flew through the air to make another acrobatic save. Spectators, who deliberately stood directly behind the goal were often rewarded with a one-man circus as Matthews went through his repertoire.

That repertoire included much more than simply keeping goal. It included clobbering a least one opposing forward per game, sometimes several at the same time, for if ever a harder goalkeeper put on a pair of gloves, I'm glad I didn't meet him. No prisoners were taken in crowded goalmouths. His own defenders often bore painful testimony to that, when they got in his way. He was also, apparently, fearless. Plunging saves at the feet of opposing forwards made spectators wince, and he had plenty of opportunity for that while playing in a side which had distinct defensive frailties. Whatever else you got with Matthews, you got good value for your money and Rams supporters loved him.

In training he was a nightmare. He liked to play 'out' in five-a-sides, especially in the Baseball Hotel car park. He was hopeless, really, and used to gallop around, as friend and foe tried desperately to avoid getting near him. One of those bony knees could put you out of action for a month. The result was that he rather fancied himself at centre-forward and thought 'playing out' was rather an easy business, not at all like goalkeeping.

He worried. He was probably the most highly-strung performer I've ever seen before a match. Woe betide anyone who accidentally disturbed his kit on its place just at the entrance to the showers and toilets. Ten minutes before kick-off he'd disappear into there, to have a fag. Even trainer Ralph Hann, a stickler for discipline, was sensible enough to turn a blind eye at that stage of the proceedings. Then the bell would sound and the slightly stooping, sallow-faced, angular figure would be transformed into a lithe, explosive performer.

Harry Storer first signed him for Coventry City and he played five times for England whilst still a Third Division South player. He joined Chelsea in 1956, for a record transfer fee for a goalkeeper, and Storer signed him again, for Derby County, in 1961. He made 246 appearances for the Rams before, aged 36, he called it a day at the end of Brian Clough's first season. After Matthews retired, a few centre-forwards slept a little more soundly in their beds.

Albert Mays – that back pass!

ALBERT Mays, born in the Rhondda Valley, was a fine all-round sportsman, a character – and a good footballer. His father had been a Welsh international and many worse players played for Wales than Albert Mays, who was a stylish wing-half in the 1950s. Mays played 281 times for the Rams, but unfortunately, is mostly remembered for a dreadful back-pass in the snow, in an FA Cup match against Preston North End in 1959. Preston were in Division One and Derby County were in Division Two, but the magic of the FA Cup caught the imagination of the public.

The crowd at the Baseball Ground was 29,237 and late in the second half, a splendid and unexpected home victory loomed. Then, with no danger threatening and acres of space and plenty of time to do anything he liked, Mays received the ball just inside his own half. To the horror of everyone, he inexplicably turned and volleyed the ball back towards goalkeeper Ken Oxford. Agonisingly, the ball slowed in the snow. Preston centre-forward Dennis Hatsell, coming back from an offside position, couldn't believe his luck. He slipped in the equaliser, the match ended 2-2 and Preston won the replay 4-2. Mays never lived that back-pass down.

It's strange how such incidents lodge in the memory. Even now, when Mays's name comes up in conversation, it's always mentioned. Then, with Mays being very much a part of the local sporting scene during the next 20 years – on the cricket field, where he was good enough to play for Derbyshire 2nd X1; on the snooker circuit, where he was Derbyshire champion more than once; in the snooker hall in Babington Lane, in which he was a partner for a while; and in the Exchange public house, where he became the licensee – the topic of conversation so often turned to that dreadful back-pass. It haunted him. A whole career measured by one pass? It isn't fair, because Albert Mays was a much better player than that.

He made his debut in 1949 and was a member of the side that slid from Division One into the Third Division North in the mid 1950s. He was also a regular member of the side that gained promotion back to Division Two in 1956-57, when his cultured, attacking style, contributed to Derby County's free-scoring displays. His passing was crisp and his support of the player on the ball was always evident. Some were critical of his defensive capabilities, but although he might have lacked a little enthusiasm for some aspects of that part of the game, he could certainly put his foot in, especially when his Celtic temper was roused.

It was roused the day he came off his mat. 'Crab' football was usually played on Friday mornings, after training, in the small gymnasium which stood where the club offices were eventually sited. It could be quite a dangerous game and there was usually a groundstaff lad stationed to keep a look-out for Ralph Hann, who was the trainer. Goalkeepers could only handle the ball if they were on their mat, but Mays liked to come off his mat to clear any loose ball. One morning, unfortunately, he kicked the wall bars. He was in agony, but no-one dared tell Ralph, or Harry Storer. He played the next day. The following week, he went for an X-ray. He'd broken his toe. Mays was always one of life's great moaners. He moaned a bit then.

Albert Mays died from cancer, tragically young, aged 44 in July 1973.

Jimmy Methven – player and manager

JIMMY Methven was one of the select few who played for Derby County and then became the club's manager. His career spanned the end of the 19th and the beginning of the 20th centuries and also World War One. A Scot, he was born in Perth in 1868 but spent the majority of his life in England and he died in Derby in 1953. Methven joined Derby County in 1891, three years after the Football League was formed. In that year penalty-kicks were introduced for the first time. It was thought necessary because of a blatant handling of the ball on the goal-line by a Notts County player in an FA Cup quarter-final against Stoke, which prevented a goal. Before then it was assumed that all handling offences were accidental. It was after all, called 'football'.

Methven was a chunky right-back known as 'Logie' because he arrived at Derby from Edinburgh St Bernard's, who played at Logie Park. In his first five seasons with the Rams he didn't miss a match and he also played in the first three of Derby County's FA Cup Finals, in 1898, 1899 and 1903, although all three were lost. Known as a clever tackler, he was a robust player who took pride in being able to 'look after himself' on the field. He was on the fringes of the Scotland team before he came to Derby County, being named as reserve when Scotland played England in 1890, but he never made the full international team, possibly because he played all his club football in England.

He might not have joined Derby, but Burton Swifts instead. Swifts were in the Second Division – Burton once boasted two Football League clubs – but the contract included running an hotel and his wife did not fancy it. Instead his first match in Derby County's colours came in the pre-season public practice match on 26 August 1891. The 'Probables' versus 'Possibles', 'Reds' v 'Blues', or other such label, was always a significant occasion for all professional clubs, until well into the 1960s. It gave supporters the chance to witness any new signings and it gave those players not in the first team a chance to challenge publicly those who were – and kick them a bit, too. The public practice match also offered a clue to the manager's thinking about his best team. When, for the first time ever, Billy Wright found Stan Cullis had named him in the 'Possibles' rather than the 'Probables' in the public practice match at Wolverhampton Wanderers, at the start of season 1959-60, he retired from the game.

When Methven made his appearance on that Wednesday evening in 1891, a pale, thin, ghost-like figure appeared at outside-right for the 'Possibles'. It was 17-year-old Steve Bloomer. Methven went on to play in, or manage, all but 19 of Bloomer's games for Derby County, so he was better placed than most to observe, at first hand the great man's talents.

Methven played his last home League game on 6 October 1906, just short of his 38th birthday, and he appeared wearing his Scottish representative cap! In August he had taken over from Harry Newbould as Derby County's first recognised full-time manager. Before then, managers combined their duties with that of secretary and many clubs continued that practice until well into the 1950s, Eric Taylor at Sheffield Wednesday being a notable example. In the first season of Methven's managership, the Rams were relegated. Part of the reason was that Bloomer was sold to Middlesbrough, but he returned in 1910 and the Rams were promoted in 1911-12. They continued to be a yo-yo team under Methven, being relegated in 1914 and 1921 and promoted in 1914-15. Methven remained manager until 1922, when he underwent an unsuccessful eye operation for glaucoma. He left quietly and his job was advertised.

He never had full control of team matters. As at most clubs, the directors often picked the team and bought and sold players. But he did oversee an early British (and probably world) record transfer when the Rams paid £2,500 for Manchester City's Horace Barnes in October 1908, to equal the record. And players were mostly signed on his recommendation because his son recalled lying in bed in the early hours at the family's home in New Normanton and hearing his father's return from scouting trips.

In all Jimmy Methven served Derby County as player and manager for 31 years, although when football was suspended in World War One he went to work at Rolls-Royce for the duration. Another son played once for the Rams, in the relegation season of 1913-14, under his father's managership.

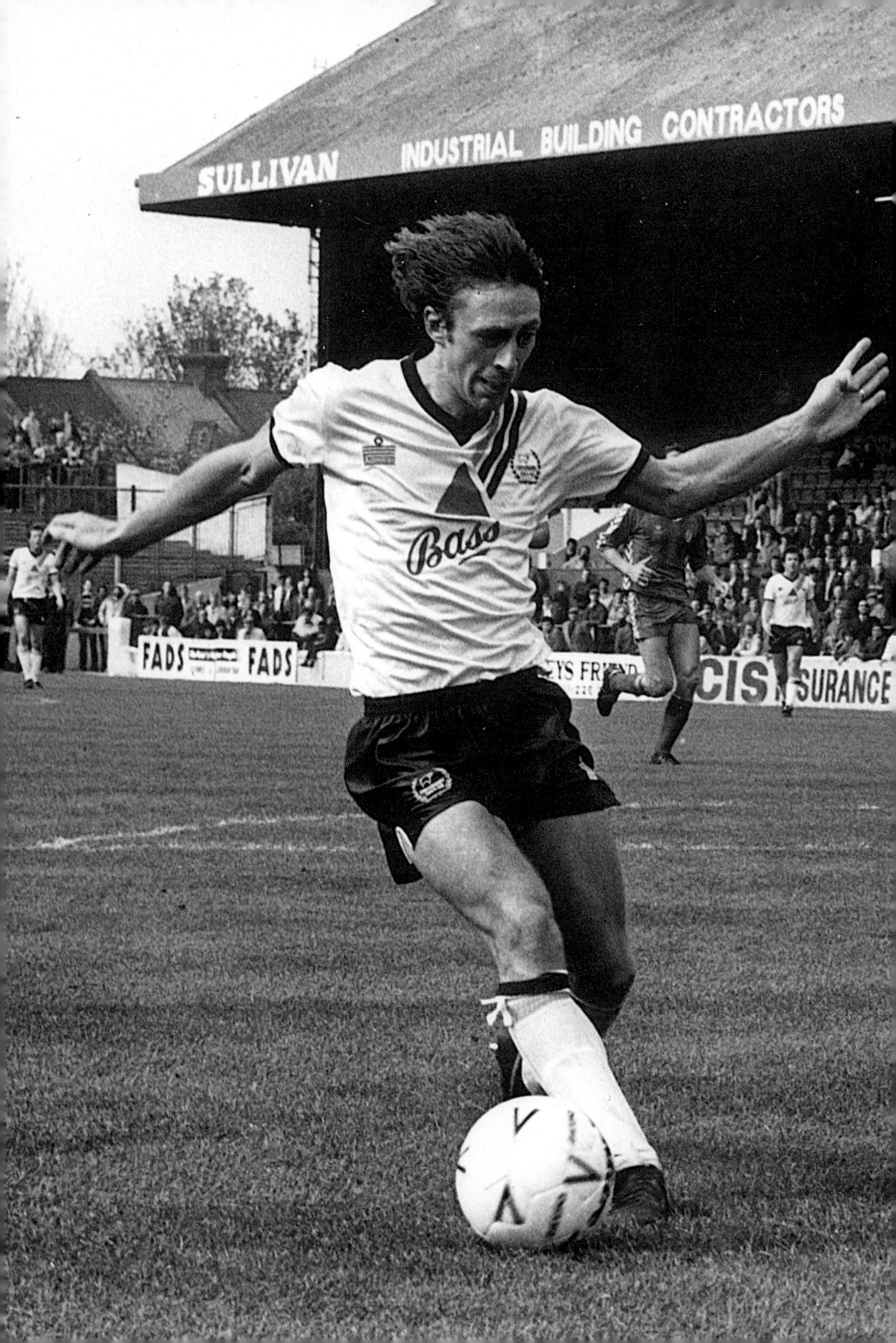
SULLIVAN
INDUSTRIAL BUILDING CONTRACTORS
FADS
FADS
Bass

Gary Micklewhite – multi-purpose footballer

IN the late 1970s, Gary Micklewhite was an apprentice at Manchester United and he signed professional forms for the club on his 17th birthday in March 1978. Tommy Docherty was manager of United when Micklewhite was an apprentice, but Docherty was sacked in July 1977 after he announced that he was leaving his wife and four children to live with Mary Brown, the wife of physiotherapist Laurie Brown. Dave Sexton took over as United manager and Docherty left Old Trafford to quickly resurface – as manager of Derby County in September 1977. He succeeded Colin Murphy.

Docherty's tenure of office was a stormy one, with players coming and going so quickly that it was suggested that a revolving door be fitted to the players' entrance at the Baseball Ground. Docherty himself didn't stay long at Derby and in May 1979 he resigned to become manager of Queen's Park Rangers. That's when he signed Gary Micklewhite from his former club, Manchester United. The 'Doc' may have had a short fuse, but he had a long memory for players and as Micklewhite was born in Southwark, moving to London was probably no hardship.

Micklewhite made 106 League appearance for the London club and also appeared in the replay of the 1982 FA Cup Final, when Tottenham Hotspur beat Queen's Park Rangers 1-0. He signed for Derby County in February 1985, a deal which was financed by the sale of Kevin Wilson to Ipswich Town. Manager Arthur Cox also secured centre-forward Trevor Christie at the same time.

By upbringing and inclination, Micklewhite was an inside-forward, or central midfield player, as they were beginning to be called. At Derby, however, he was regarded as a right winger, or wide right midfielder. What it really boiled down to was that Micklewhite was a good footballer who could fulfil a muti-purpose role and his contribution to two promotions and Derby County's resurgence under Cox was considerable. Whatever else you got with Micklewhite, you could be sure of a consistent and wholehearted performance, although that is really damning him with faint praise. Micklewhite was rather a better player than that and it was easy to underrate him. A succession of centre-forwards, from Bobby Davison to Mick Harford, would vouch for the service they got from the right-hand side, whilst full-backs like Mel Sage and midfielders like George Williams and John Gregory had reason to appreciate his good positioning, availability to receive the ball and sheer hard work. Micklewhite, more than anything was 'a players' player'. Not as quick as Steve Coppell, or as clever as Martin O'Neill, or having the sheer quality of Ian Callaghan, Micklewhite fulfilled a similar role and was a worthy successor in Derby County's colours to John McGovern.

He was twice an ever-present in a Football League season for Derby County, in two promotions seasons 1985-86 and 1986-87, and in that period joined a rare band of only ten Derby County players who have made 100 consecutive League appearances. Overall, he played 257 times for Derby County, plus 20 as a substitute, and scored a useful 43 goals. Micklewhite and Nigel Callaghan, Micklewhite and McMinn. Wingers incorporated.

Johnny Morris – he wriggled and slithered

IN the immediate post-war years of the 1940s, Derby County were one of the biggest-spending clubs in English football. Twice they broke the British transfer record, the first time when the signed Billy Steel, for £15,500 from Morton in 1947, the second when they signed Johnny Morris, for £24,500 from Manchester United in 1949. Both were sparky characters and they made 43 appearances together for Derby County, but in Carter and Doherty, they had a hard act to follow.

What sort of players were they, Morris and Steel? Reg Harrison on Morris: "Johnny Morris was a good passer of the ball. He was a good player, but he hung on, sometimes, too long. You'd make two, or three moves, go one way and you wouldn't get the ball, go the other way and you wouldn't get the ball. You'd think, 'Oh, where can I go?' Then it comes and perhaps you don't want it then. He was a good player, though, no doubt about that." Morris on Steel: "Well, he was a typical Scottish player. Yes, a dribbler. He used to run himself into the ground. He was the type of lad you can't play with. They had one at Liverpool, now Real Madrid, McManaman. Nice lad, Billy, but football?"

Morris went on to play 140 games for Derby County, scoring 47 goals and winning three England caps. He had played in the 1948 FA Cup Final, when Manchester United beat Blackpool 4-1 in what it is claimed was the best-ever Wembley Final, a sheer feast of football. Derby County were in the semi-final that year, Manchester United beat them, 3-1 at Hillsborough, but all was not happy in the United camp. It was alleged that the Derby players were on £100 per man to win. Illegal, of course. At that time the maximum wage was £14 per week, but in 1941 four Derby County directors were suspended *sine die* for making illegal payments in the 1930s.

Morris was one of the militant United players who persuaded captain Johnny Carey to approach manager Matt Busby to see if United would match the Derby payment. Busby refused. Said Morris, "Of course, we got nothing extra at United, but what I am sure he [someone who made a comment after the game] meant that Derby were on some extra. They were well known for perks at that time." It was the beginning of an uneasy relationship between Morris and Busby which culminated in Morris being put on the transfer list and signing for Derby County.

There is no doubt that Derby County had 'sounded out' Morris long before he was eventually transferred. Said Morris, "I was approached at Manchester United by a certain person and he gave me a letter with a phone number. It was a year before I rang, but I always knew there was a club there, but I didn't know which club it was. I'd got an idea, though, because the person who gave me this letter was an old Derby County player!"

In his book *A Strange Kind Of Glory*, Eamon Dunphy writes: 'Busby could never fathom Morris out, he subsequently confided to an earlier biographer: "I've tried every angle. I've bullied, I've used flattery. I've tried every way, but I just can't get through." Morris was a talented man, intelligent, of independent disposition, who possessed convictions about his rights and the true nature of professional football which were correct and not amenable to 'flattery' or 'bullying', to paternalism or authoritarianism.'

Matters came to a head shortly before the FA Cup semi-final, in 1949, when Manchester United were due to play Wolverhampton Wanderers. Morris had been injured and when he was fit, Busby didn't put him straight back in the first team. One day, during training, Busby called him out in front of the other players for not trying. Morris responded that it wasn't worth bothering with for reserve matches and began to walk off to the dressing- rooms. Busby called after him: "If you walk off this pitch, you'll never kick a ball for this club again." Morris ignored him. Busby went to his office, telephoned the Press Association news agency and informed them that Morris was on the transfer list. The news was given to Morris by a journalist. Three days before the semi-final took place, Morris was transferred to Derby County. The semi-final was drawn 1-1 and Wolves won the replay 1-0. Most people in Manchester believed that had Morris played, United would have won.

In December 1950, Jack Lee scored four in Derby's 6-5 win over Sunderland, on an icy snow-bound Baseball Ground pitch. But the real star of the show was Johnny Morris. Said the *Derby Evening Telegraph*: 'Morris wriggled and slithered through the Sunderland defence with a speed which would have put Rudolph the Red-Nosed Reindeer to shame.' Derby were in decline when he was transferred to Leicester City in 1952, and he played more than 200 games for them, helping win the Second Division title in 1954.

Bert Mozley – football was fun

BERT Mozley was born on 23 September 1923 at 33 Old Chester Road, Derby. He is Derby's only born and bred England player. Nowadays he lives in Canada, on the idyllic Galiano Island in British Columbia. It's a long way from Chester Green where he learned to play football with his elder brother Cliff. Mozley recalls those days with great pleasure: "My first pair of 'footers' were an old pair of black boots. My Dad brought some cogs and nailed these on to the soles. To me, the sound of those studs as they hit the pavement was the best sound in the world. I really felt grown-up. I believe I was around four years old at the time."

His first trophy was gained when St Paul's won the Derby Schoolboys Cup in 1937. After that match, he went home on the bus with his mum, clutching the small silver cup which for many years had pride of place on the mantelpiece. When he left school he joined Rolls-Royce as an apprentice, but because he suffered a nasty thigh muscle injury, he was prevented from playing football for two years at a most crucial stage of a young player's development. Later he joined Shelton United and was 'spotted' by Nottingham Forest and played several games in their junior teams. At that time he was playing as an inside-forward, but Derby County scouts were also watching Shelton United. After one particular match a man approached young Mozley and suggested he would be better suited to playing right-back. The man was former Rams star Jack Bowers and Mozley took his advice. He progressed through the Rams junior teams and signed professional forms in 1945. Ted Magner was the manager and his words had a lasting effect on Mozley: "Bert, one day you will be playing before thousands of fans. All I need from you is your best effort. You have the skills and where else is there a job going that pays you to keep fit." The following day, Mozley got married.

Mozley never forgot Magner's words. He took up weight training, one of the first players to do so and against the wishes of the club, which thought he would become 'muscle-bound'. Mozley, however, studied the science of using weights to the extent that later in life he won many body-building contests in Canada. Now, nearly 78 years old, he still works out daily and has converted a garage at his home on Galiano Island into a gymnasium, where up to 30 people go to train regularly with him. If you catch him on one of his visits to Derby, it will invariably be at one of the health clubs in town. "Just keeping ticking over," will be his cheerful greeting. He looks about 50 and recently underwent a knee operation. "I was on the operating table when the doc said, 'Get me this man's records. I've got the wrong chap. This isn't the body of a man in his 70s!'"

He played in an era which today's players would find hard to imagine. When the Rams played in London, against Arsenal, Chelsea, Spurs, Mozley would be waiting near his Allestree home for the Derby Corporation bus to the railway station and would regularly see Oswald Jackson, a director, drive past him to catch the same train. Jackson would wave, but there was never the slightest possibility that a director would stop to give a lift to one of the club's players, even if that player was an England international and even if they were both going to the same game.

Mozley played 321 matches for Derby County and won three England caps. He also toured Canada with an FA XI in 1950 and it was probably on that tour that he fell in love with the country. He played his last match for the Rams in 1954. The following year, he emigrated. Calm in possession, quick in recovery and with great energy, Mozley was also the joker of the dressing-room. A young Jack Parry, just starting his career, probably picked up a few tips from Mozley in that department. Bert Mozley is still smiling. It's no surprise his autobiography is entitled *When Football was Fun*.

Chick Musson – is he playing today?

CHICK Musson was one of three locally-born players to win FA Cup winners' medals in 1946. The other two were Jack Nicholas and Reg Harrison. Chick was born William Urban Musson at Kilburn in 1920 and why he was known as 'Chick' is somewhat of a mystery. "I shared a room with him for seven years," says Reg Harrison, "but I've no idea why he was called Chick." What is not in any doubt is that many opposition forwards probably called him something else during the 280 matches he played for Derby County as a wing-half between 1945-1953, for people will tell you that Chick Musson was hard. Bone-crunchingly hard. Shudderingly hard. Hard.

Musson was the type of player who tended to occupy the thoughts of opponents on the night before a match. "Is Chick playing today?" they'd enquire hesitatingly when they got the ground. Also, in the dressing-room, getting changed. Team talks do not centre around this sort of player very much. Managers tend to focus on opposition players of a more artistic persuasion, when indulging in tactics, or the modern equivalent, the game plan. Individuals, however, who happen to play in the area of the pitch where this type of player operated, are inclined to take other things into consideration. They look at things a shade more seriously, than if they were playing against a different type of opponent of, let us say, a milder reputation. Making physical contact with players like Chick Musson could be most unpleasant. His business was tackling, hard. Opponents knew it.

Musson was only about 5ft 7ins tall, but he was solidly built. Tim Ward: "He tackled standing up, his shoulders sloping and his chest sticking out in front. You just didn't tackle his foot. You tackled twelve stone of him. All of him. Chick was a wonderful character and a lot better player than a lot of people gave him credit for. He was a hard player, probably one of the hardest players in football at that time, but a great man to have in your side. Chick was never beaten."

He joined Derby County from Holbrook St. Michael's as a 15-year-old amateur in 1936. Players had to be 17 years of age before they could turn professional and he did so as soon as he was able and played mainly in the Reserves and 'A' teams before the war. He made one first-team appearance, in 1943, but after that played more regularly until by the time the FA Cup run started, he was a fixture in the side at left-half, although he did miss the first tie, against Luton Town. Tim Ward wore the number-six shirt in the first leg at Kenilworth Road and in the second leg, at the Baseball Ground, Tommy Eggleston made his only appearance for Derby County. Musson then took over, up to and including Wembley.

In 1946-47, football returned to normal after the war years and in the following five seasons, Musson, oddly, missed only one League match in each season. Was he superstitious? He played in 205 League matches out of a possible 210 and his consistency of performance was a byword. He was also consistent in respect of goalscoring. He never did. Not a single goal in his entire career. As a defensive wing-half, his business was tackling – and business was business. Neither did he earn international honours, although he did play for the Football League versus the Irish League, in 1950 in Belfast.

He eventually left Derby County at the end of season 1952-53, to become player-manager of Brush Sports at Loughborough. They were members of the Birmingham League. He soon became ill with a blood disorder and in April 1955, aged 34, Chick Musson died of leukemia. At his funeral the coffin was borne in by Jack Stamps, Bill Townsend, Ken Oliver and Leon Leuty. Eight months later, aged 35, Leuty died also.

Henry Newton – high cruising speed

HENRY Newton was an all-purpose, dynamo-type of a player. Not tall, but strong and compact, Newton was a fierce competitor who made it hard work for opponents. He could tackle hard, challenge for everything in the air and pick up the pieces all over the place. In horse racing parlance, he had 'a high cruising speed', which means he could run forever. Yet Newton seemed to be underrated. What people often didn't see was that Newton was good at doing the simple things well. That, in football especially, isn't easy to do.

Newton was a 29-year-old experienced professional with more than 350 League appearances under his belt when Brian Clough signed him for Derby County, from Everton in September 1973. He'd actually been a transfer target for Clough and Taylor during his Nottingham Forest days. He was born in Nottingham and was an apprentice at the City Ground before signing professional forms in 1961. The majority of his career was spent with Forest, for whom he made a total of 315 appearances and he won four England under-23 international caps. He also played for the Football League.

Newton was Clough and Taylor's last signing before they left the Baseball Ground a month later, in October 1973. When a manager leaves a club, the new manager often changes things around, but Dave Mackay resisted that temptation, for a while. Then he signed Bruce Rioch at the end of February, and Newton relinquished his hold on the number-four shirt. He still made 18 League appearances that season, but if he feared for his place the following season, his fears proved to be unfounded. He played 35 League games in 1974-75, sharing the midfield role with Archie Gemmill and Bruce Rioch as Derby County carried off the championship for the second time. It was a topsy-turvy season. The Rams didn't go to the top of the League until early April and it was a season when six different teams led the table by December. In all, the lead changed hands during the season a record 21 times. At the other end of the table, Chelsea were relegated and Tottenham Hotspur only survived by beating Leeds United on the last day of the season. Manchester United were promoted from Division Two with an average attendance of 48,388.

The following season Newton played in the European Cup, in the epic battles with Real Madrid. Having taken part in the pulsating tie at the Baseball Ground, when the Rams won 4-1, Newton also played in the second match in the Bernabeau Stadium in front of a crowd of 120,000, the biggest that Derby County have experienced. Both he and Roy McFarland played with pain-killing injections, Francis Lee was suspended and the Rams were beaten 5-1, after extra-time.

After Mackay left, Newton played a few matches at left-back under Colin Murphy's management, but his appearances became less frequent and he left Derby County in 1977, to play for Walsall where he stayed for only a brief period before retiring from the game after battling with injuries. He played a total of 149 matches for Derby County, plus seven as a substitute. Like many former players, arthritis became a problem, but it didn't prevent him becoming a proficient golfer, when he was able to take time away from running his sub-Post Office at the Cavendish, which he did for 20 years.

Jack Nicholas – the man who lifted the Cup

IF ever a player could be called durable, it would be Jack Nicholas. Between 16 September 1931 until the day war broke out in September 1939, Derby County played 356 League and FA Cup matches. Nicholas missed only four, of which three were League matches and one was in the FA Cup. It is an amazing record. He never played for England, or the Football League, he just played for Derby County. It was fitting that he was captain of the side that won the FA Cup in 1946 and he led by example.

Jimmy Bullions recalls, "I'll always remember Jack Nicholas saying to me, 'At corner-kicks, I'm going to watch [Don] Welch.' Jack was a big bustler. He said: 'You take [Chris] Duffy, if he's not taking the corners on that side. Or one of the other players.' Well, that took a lot of pressure off me, because Welch was big and strong and good in the air and it was a bit of a worry."

Nicholas played only nine matches the following season, 1946-47, before retiring. He made a total of 383 appearances in peacetime, to which could be added a considerable number during the war years when he also helped run the club after it started up again late in 1941. He was an ever-present in four separate seasons for Derby County.

Nicholas was brought up in football. His father, Jack senior, played for Derby County as a right-back, taking over from Jimmy Methven when Methven stepped up to become manager in 1906. Jack senior moved to Swansea Town in 1912, two years after young Jack was born in Derby. Young Jack grew up in Swansea and won schoolboy international honours for Wales, but when the family returned to Derby, he joined Derby County's groundstaff as a 16-year-old right-half.

He grew up to be a strong, tough, 6ft-plus, right-footed player, without frills. He wasn't a crowd favourite either. "I never reckoned him a footballer,' said Alf Jeffries. "Well, he wasn't a footballer. The crowd used to get at him: 'Go on Jack. Kick it anywhere.' And he would kick it over the stand, if it would please them. He managed, though. He carried on, all them games and played in the Cup Final and was captain, wasn't he?" He was indeed. By this time he was playing at right-back. Jimmy Bullions again: "Jack was a smashing fellow to get on with. He was stern and all the rest of it. In fact when I went from Chesterfield to Derby, he didn't speak to me for quite some time. I went to play right-half and Jack had, kind of, being running Derby. After the war started they'd got no manager until Ted Magner came. Jack felt I was going to shove him out, but they moved him to right-back and it wasn't until he'd played right-back for a bit that he started talking to me."

In fact Derby County closed down for the first two years of the war and a number of players, including Nicholas, went as guest players to Notts County. Nicholas joined the Derby Borough Police Force and, playing at centre-forward, once scored all four goals against Nottingham Borough Police. When Derby County resumed operations on Christmas Day 1941, against an RAF XI at the Baseball Ground, Nicholas acted as temporary manager, before Ted Magner was appointed in 1944.

Nicholas scored a total of 16 goals for Derby County and was an occasional penalty-taker. He scored the only goal, from the penalty spot, when Derby County beat Aston Villa 1-0 at the Baseball Ground, the day before war was declared in 1939. That goal was expunged from the records, but when the League restarted for the 1946-47 season, the same 1939-40 fixture list was used. Ironically, Nicholas was carried off with a knee injury in the repeat Aston Villa game. The Rams lost 2-1.

Of course, Jack Nicholas's greatest moment was receiving the FA Cup from King George VI in 1946. Pictures show Nicholas carrying the Cup down the staircase from the Royal Box; on the shoulders of teammates around the ground at Wembley; on top of the open-topped coach around the streets of Derby. You don't see many photographs of anyone else holding the Cup itself. Derby County have appeared in four FA Cup Finals, but Nicholas has, so far, been the only captain to be presented with the trophy. All the evidence suggests that, in 1946, he didn't intend letting go.

David Nish – he had time

IF Raich Carter carried empty space around with him like an umbrella, David Nish had the time. Calm and unhurried, Nish picked his way around the top flight of English football like a man on his way to the office. Along the way he made 233 appearances, plus four as substitute for Derby County, played five times for England, won a League championship medal in 1975 and played in Europe. There was also the little matter of the British record transfer fee (£225,000) it took for Brian Clough to persuade Leicester City to part with a player who, at 21 years of age, had captained them in the 1969 FA Cup Final. Sadly, a serious knee injury eventually brought a premature end to a cultured career.

Describing Nish, the player to a complete stranger could be difficult. Especially if that person was a football manager, or coach. You would have to explain that the right-footed Nish was a left-back who didn't kick the ball with his left foot very often. He wasn't quick; he didn't dominate in the air; and no, he didn't tackle too much either. Sliding tackles were definitely not part of his repertoire, such desperate measures he probably treated with aristocratic disdain. Yet, with all these unfavourable characterisics lying around, Harry Storer's eternal question always comes to mind, drifting along on the wind: "Yes, yes, I know all of that, but CAN HE PLAY?" And you'd reply. "Oh yes. This boy can play. Like a prince."

One of the key components that separates good teams from the rest is the ability to play the ball out accurately from the back. Long or short, it requires good footballers to do that. Defenders need a clear picture of the field of play before the ball arrives, which means the ball can then be played early. That, in turn, gives midfielders and forwards a brief second of extra time. Nish could do that and often did, but he also liked to hold the ball. When he did that, it became a master class in how to manoeuvre a football, to create an opening. Along the wing he'd lope, then he'd check inside. Head up, elegant, manoeuvring the ball with his right foot, playing a game of bluff with the opposing defenders as to when he was going to release it. "Release it, release it," you'd cry, inwardly. "Now, now, for goodness sake" – and he'd manoeuvre it a touch more, like a fastidious aunt arranging a vase of flowers on the sideboard. Then, suddenly, it was gone, often with the defender on the wrong foot and Charlie George, Alan Hinton, or Archie Gemmill in a better position than they, or anyone else, had ever imagined.

What about those fast right wingers, though? Well, strangely, they never really seemed to get much success. Not many headers were scored against Derby County on the back post, either. Inevitably, tackles were needed sometimes, especially in crowded penalty areas. It was then that Nish would put a firm foot in and emerge with the ball, calmly, with dignity, oblivious to the fuss around him – and always, always, with time, plenty of time, to spare.

If he has one bitter memory from football it is the 1976 FA Cup semi-final at Hillsborough. Manchester United were leading through a Gordon Hill goal when Nish collected the ball, put it back over the onrushing defenders and then strolled through to regain it and shoot. "You assume that no-one else can be interfering with play if you play the ball yourself. But unfortunately the ref gave somebody offside on the other side of the pitch. I couldn't believe it... had I been able to equalise – and I don't even know if the ball was in the net before the ref blew – then anything could have happened. But, of course, Gordon Hill scored again, a deflection. It just typified my day really."

John O'Hare – a great target man

JOHN O'Hare had never seen the Baseball Ground when he joined Derby County in 1967. In fact, he'd never been to Derby in his life. Now, it seems now as though he's never been anywhere else, and it is significant that he has lived in the area since the day he signed. Nevertheless, despite his great affection for Derby County, the city and the people, you still sense in O'Hare a deep loyalty to Sunderland. You can take the boy out of the place, but you can't take the place out of the boy. So it should be. If O'Hare had to leave Wearside to be properly appreciated elsewhere, it didn't mean he fell out with his first League club, the side he'd joined as a youngster after beginning his career with Drumchapel Amateurs.

He'd played 51 League matches and scored 14 goals when Brian Clough went back to his former club to sign the centre-forward, who was a month short of his 21st birthday. Clough began his coaching career as youth-team coach at Sunderland and O'Hare was one of his protégés. It was Clough's first signing as Derby County manager, the transfer fee was £20,000, but it took supporters some time before they began to appreciate O'Hare. For a start it was easy to identify qualities he didn't have. He wasn't very quick; he wasn't a dribbler; he wasn't outstanding in the air; he wasn't even a prolific goalscorer; he wasn't an eye catcher; or a crowd pleaser. For a while, he certainly didn't please the majority of the crowd at the Baseball Ground.

Gradually, however, supporters began to appreciate the things he could do and how well he did them. Like receiving the ball out of defence and holding it brilliantly until support arrived. Like his superb positional play which made it easy for colleagues, in defence and midfield, to find him with a pass from deep positions. Ron Webster: "John O'Hare was always there. Whenever I got it, I could always hit John O'Hare, no matter what. He just seemed to be there and if you hit him a bad ball he'd get to it, he'd get it down and whatever and they'd feed off him, wouldn't they?" Kevin Hector agrees: "If the ball went up there, it stuck. I used to drop off defenders and go a bit wide and they didn't know whether to come or stay. He was strong and held the ball up so well and they couldn't knock him off it."

It sounds so simple, doesn't it? So why didn't – and don't – other players and teams play like that? Gordon Hughes has the answer: "I used to try that when I used to coach, but it didn't work. There wasn't a John O'Hare, you see! It used to be bouncing off chests and going away. You've got to have the right chap to do it and I though he was a great target man, John O'Hare."

He made a total of 305 appearances (plus three sub) for Derby County and scored 81 goals and he also won 13 caps for Scotland. He won a League championship medal at Derby County and at Nottingham Forest and his final match was when he came on as a substitute in Forest's second European Cup success, against Hamburg, in Madrid in 1980.

If he hobbles a bit these days, it's because his ankles are not what they were, the penalty of being a centre-forward in an era when tackling from the back was allowed. It makes you wince to think of it, but O'Hare missed only four League games in his first five season at Derby. Said Brian Clough: "He had the biggest heart in England."

Ken Oxford – an old-fashioned goalkeeper

THE 'Ox', as he was universally known, joined Derby County from Norwich City in December 1957. He'd had a trial for the Rams nine years earlier, but he wasn't engaged. He'd played one match for Manchester City against Arsenal in the First Division and kept a clean sheet, but it wasn't enough to keep him at Maine Road, hardly surprising when one considers that Frank Swift was the regular 'keeper. Neither did he have any success at Chesterfield, Ray Middleton keeping him out of the side. He kept trying and moved on, to Norwich where he understudied Ken Nethercott and then replaced him. He made 136 appearances for Norwich City before Harry Storer signed him to replace Terry Webster.

I always think of the 'Ox' as being one of the last of the breed of goalkeepers who wore those heavy woollen roll-necked jumpers that must have weighed a ton when they got wet. Those jumpers were often accompanied by a large, everyday sort of flat cap, which they threw casually into the back of the goal before being peppered with shots before kick-off. Those jumpers and caps often framed stern-looking faces, which peered out from grainy black and white head-and-shoulders photographs, in magazines like *Soccer Star* and publications like *The FA Book for Boys* and *Charles Buchan's Football Annual*. Old-fashioned they were and the 'Ox' was an old-fashioned sort of goalkeeper. He was not spectacular, he relied on good positioning, but he was strong, solid and usually safe – except when he hit his head on the goalpost.

Goalkeepers of that era used to keep goal from the goal-line much more than modern goalkeepers. There were good reasons for that as in heavy goalmouths it wasn't possible to do a lot of rushing about. The back-pass law wasn't in operation, centre-halves were expected to dominate high balls into the penalty area, and the shoulder-charging of goalkeepers was still not completely outlawed. Whatever the reasons, the 'Ox' tended to stay at home, which was fine until a high ball to the far post would see him, usually once a season, backing furiously along his goal line and colliding with the back post. If he connected with his head, Jack Parry went in goal – no substitutes then – and sometime later the 'Ox' would appear on the touchline ready to trundle up and down the right wing. Like all goalkeepers, he fancied his chances when 'playing out' and we sometimes wondered whether or not he was really fit to resume, or was still in a daze. You couldn't tell from the way he played. He always 'played out' like that in training.

Like Reg Matthews, who Storer signed to replace him in November 1961, the 'Ox' liked a 'fag'. In fact, he liked one rather a lot and Jack Parry used to joke that when the 'Ox' went off injured and he had to deputise in goal, he used to collect the 'nub ends' that were stubbed out at the foot of the post.

Seriously, Ken Oxford was a good professional and if he wasn't the best goalkeeper Derby County ever had, he was probably the bravest. Forwards through on goal could be sure there would be no desperate diving, or going to ground early from the 'Ox'. He used to crouch slightly and face the ball and the music. Often a fierce drive, from point-blank range, would rebound off him like a tennis ball off a brick wall – and the 'Ox' never flinched. He left Derby County for Doncsater Rovers in July 1964, after 162 appearances, and later played and managed in non-League football. He loved the game and was still playing in a local Sunday morning league and for the Ex-Rams team, well into his 50s, still diving headlong into the boots.

He became a Securicor guard and on one occasion foiled an armed robbery attempt in Ilkeston. Those who played with the 'Ox' would have expected no less. When he died in **1993** there was a particular air of sadness among those who knew him.

Jack Parry – joker in the pack

JACK Parry played more League matches than anyone else in Derby County's history – 482 plus one as substitute. At least, he started more League matches than anyone else. Once substitutes were introduced, 'appearances' began to take the place of 'games played', although a substitute appearance can be less than a minute's duration. All players will say that having one's name in the starting XI is the thing that matters, anything else is really only consolation, whatever the 'rotationalists' and 'bench advocates' claim.

Kevin Hector, with 478 League matches started, plus eight as substitute, is now generally regarded as leading the way in the Derby County appearances list. In all matches Jack Parry is in fifth place, with 516/1. Whatever the semantics, it's safe to say that in Parry's professional career, which lasted from 1948 to 1965 (he wasn't actually released until 1967), there were plenty of laughs along the way. For Jack Parry was one of life's great wits and stories of his quick ripostes are multifarious.

"See if there's a letter for me," was the voice from the back of the team coach when an argument with a Post Office van on the way to a match at Rotherham left letters and parcels strewn all over the place. "Can't do a thing, Ralph," came the answer to lugubrious trainer Ralph Hann, at half-time in a match against Grimsby Town. "This Cockerill is perching all over me." And when trainer Hann applied cold water to rouse a concussed Parry and asked him if he knew where he was, Jack opened one eye and replied, "We're at Wembley, we're beating Brazil 2-0 – and I've got 'em both."

Jack Parry was quick with the words and quick with his feet. As might be expected by someone who began as a winger, Parry was of average build and really sharp off the mark. He was a busy type of player and when he moved inside to become a striker, his quickness of mind and movement helped him to become leading scorer in three seasons, on his way to 110 career goals. In 34 appearances in 1955-56, he'd scored 24 League goals before a crunching tackle by Grimsby's Ray de Gruchy virtually put an end to his season. That was some collision. People talk about it still.

From about 1960 onwards, his appearances were more in midfield than attack. There, his early and simple passing meant he was easy to play with, whilst his energy was always impressive. Under Tim Ward he was an ever-present in two seasons and his constructive play had much to do with the Rams being a goalscoring side at that time. Unfortunately, they conceded too many goals as well.

Parry came from a footballing family. Four brothers went into professional football with varying degrees of success. Jack and Glyn to Derby County, Cyril to Notts County and Ray to Bolton Wanderers. Ray played in the Derby Boys' team that reached the Final of the English Schools' Shield in 1949. Future Rams Ray Young and Dennis McQuillan were colleagues. In an era when schoolboy football played at under-15 level was massively supported, 22,000 attended the second-leg at the Baseball Ground, where Derby Boys lost on aggregate to Barnsley Boys. Ray won schoolboy international honours and, in 1951, became Bolton's youngest ever debutant when he played in the top flight, against Wolverhampton Wanderers, aged 15 years 267 days. He later won two England caps.

Jack Parry liked playing football, but oddly, for someone who played so many matches, football itself didn't seem to interest him much. If the playing staff had to report for a midweek reserve match, Parry would comply and then would quite likely catch a bus home, rather than watch the match. Watching football wasn't his business. Apparently he has taken little or no interest in the game in the 30-odd years since he retired. It's each to his own, but if wit, humour, banter and quip is an essential part of team spirit, for nigh on 20 years no-one could have contributed more than Jack Parry.

Mart Poom – how many points is he worth?

IT is a schizophrenic business, goalkeeping. Huge applause for a spectacular save, downright degradation for the blunder that costs a goal. Some goalkeepers are luckier than others. Mistakes can be covered up by last-ditch scrapes off the line, or the desperate clearance of a loose ball that has slithered through the fingers like wet fish. Not all mistakes lead to losing scorelines, but although the conventional wisdom states that all goalkeepers make mistakes, which is undeniably true, some mistakes matter more than others. What matters ultimately, is 'how many'? Peter Taylor always claimed that Peter Shilton was worth ten points a season to Nottingham Forest. What Taylor, himself a former Middlesbrough goalkeeper, meant was not that Shilton would make more good saves than his rivals, but would make fewer mistakes.'

How many points is Mart Poom worth, I wonder? In his excellent book *The Soccer Syndrome*, John Moynihan wrote: 'A goalkeeper is a man on his own, based in an open box with a net, and alone with his problems.'

Poom made his debut on 5 April 1997 against Manchester United at Old Trafford, in front of a crowd of 55,243. That match, of course, will forever be remembered as Paulo Wanchope's match, but it might not have been if Poom hadn't made a couple of important early saves from headers by Ryan Giggs and Eric Cantona. That's when we first heard the sound 'Poooooooom... Pooooooooom,' rolling round the ground from where Derby County supporters were seated. It's now become a feature of Rams' games. Initially, some people, including television commentators, thought the sound was one of booing. Booing Poom? Hardly. The Estonian is one of Derby County's best-ever goalkeepers. Arguably, he is the best.

He is, certainly, the best of any goalkeeper I've ever seen at Derby, or anywhere else for that matter, at commanding the penalty area. His height helps – he is 6ft 5ins tall – but it also requires good judgment and confidence to come out for crosses as far he does. When Poom takes charge, he intimidates the opposition into trying to hit flat centres, which are often cut off before they can cause trouble.

Jim Smith signed him first for Portsmouth, but work permit problems, because of European Union regulations about 'foreign' players, forced him to return to Estonia. Smith didn't forget and when Russell Hoult went through a bad patch, which included conceding six goals at Middlesbrough in early March 1997, he went back to Estonia and FC Flora Tallinn to sign the 25-year-old goalkeeper, who was by that time an experienced international with 49 caps. It didn't go amiss either that Poom had recently performed outstandingly in a match against Scotland.

It's obvious that Poom takes goalkeeping seriously. Very seriously indeed. His training regime is intense, his self-analysis unrelenting. Nowadays, most Premiership clubs, quite rightly, employ specialist goalkeeping coaches. After all, goalkeepers are different and Poom would be the first to acknowledge the help, advice and assistance he's received from former Rams goalkeeper Eric Steele.

He gets down well for ground shots close to his body. They are the most difficult saves for all goalkeepers, especially tall men of angular build, although Poom's not adverse to using his foot to deal with such efforts, if necessary. His reactions are quick, a tribute to the long hours of practice on which he thrives, but most of all, he doesn't make many mistakes. Peter Taylor would approve. Concentration is the key to goalkeeping success. Nobody in the Premiership does it better.

Steve Powell – he was just brilliant

I FIRST saw Steve Powell play for Gayton Avenue Junior School, Littleover. Even at ten years old, his poise and composure indicated that he might become an excellent footballer and he could certainly play. He dominated the field like the great Duncan Edwards did for Manchester United in the early 1950s. As Geoffrey Green described it in *The Times*: 'Like a battleship in high seas.'

In the 1950s and 1960s, schoolboy football was highly organised and Powell went on to captain England schoolboys, but it wasn't until a boy reached school-leaving age that he was allowed to join a professional club. It meant that schoolboy internationals were prized captures. Stories of shady deals and under-the-counter payments to parents were rife. Says Powell, "Brian Clough came to the school one day, to see the headmaster, Dr Chapman. I knew what he was coming for, but hadn't said anything. So everybody was buzzing with, 'Oh, Brian Clough's been to the school today.' Nobody knew what for – until it came out in the press later."

Powell comes from a footballing family. His father, Tommy, also went to Bemrose School and he made his debut as a 16-year-old, during the war years. Tommy Powell went on to play 406 matches for Derby County in peacetime. Steve played 409 times, plus 11 as a substitute. Even Steve junior, Tommy's grandson, was on the Derby County playing staff for a while.

Says Powell, "I signed schoolboy forms when I was 14. You weren't allowed actually to play for the club until you'd left school. I left school when I had just turned 15 and, funnily enough, I played on a pre-season tour, illegally really I suppose. When I played in Germany I was technically still at school, at Bemrose Grammar School. I played on that pre-season tour and I started my apprenticeship the following summer." It's the stuff of schoolboy dreams.

Steve Powell made his debut for Derby County when he was a month past his 16th birthday. It was on a Wednesday night, against Stoke City, in a Texaco Cup-tie at the Baseball Ground in 1971. The following Saturday he was substitute, against Arsenal at Highbury. "I came on for about the last 15 minutes and then I played a full game against Nottingham Forest the Saturday after that. How old? I was just 16. I don't remember an awful lot about it, no. I remember a bit about the Liverpool game later in the season."

That was Derby County's last match of the 1971-72 season, on the evening of Monday, 1 May. Liverpool and Leeds United had a match in hand over the Rams, so it was a game that had to be won and the final match results had to fall Derby County's way. Over 39,000 packed the Baseball Ground; 3,000 Liverpool supporters were locked outside. Derby County's team was announced: 16-year-old Steve Powell, at right back.

Tommy Powell: "I was at work at the *Telegraph* and it was a night match. Somebody came up and said: 'You're wanted down in the front office.' That was the old offices. It was Brian [Clough]. He said, 'I'm playing the bairn tonight.' I said, 'You're joking, aren't you?' 'No,' he said, 'he'll be all right. I've just left them [at the Midland Hotel] and he's gone to bed.' That was it."

Steve Powell: "It was a big game for the club. They needed to win to stand any chance of winning the League. The game went very quick. At the time, I didn't feel any nerves about playing. I suppose if it had been later on in my career, it would probably have been worse, but with me being young, I just wanted to go out there and play and I enjoyed it immensely."

Gerald Mortimer wrote in the *Derby Evening Telegraph*: 'Powell was brilliant. Not brilliant for a 16-year-old; just brilliant'. Derby County won 1-0. Seven days later, both Liverpool and Leeds United failed to win. Derby County were champions. Powell played 22 League matches the following season and 29 the season after that. European Cup football and, in 1974-75, a second championship followed. He was still only 19.

Injuries took toll of his later career. That and playing in a declining side, even into the Third Division. Being versatile, perhaps, didn't help. He played in most positions but maybe he lacked an inch or so for centre-half and a yard of pace in midfield, to become a full international. Steve Powell, though, had a fine career and those boyhood dreams surely came true.

Tommy Powell – charmed us all

ONE of Tommy Powell's most treasured memories was of playing for Firs Estate Junior School in a schools' cup final on the Baseball Ground before the war. Perhaps that's where his love of the Baseball Ground began.

He used to stand outside the players' entrance for autographs and he managed to obtain Steve Bloomer's autograph. He kept that in his wallet, even as an adult, for he never lost his youthful hero worship of great players, many of whom he played with and against. "Tommy Lawton? What a player," he'd say. "Raich? A sergeant major. Peter? Up and down, up and down. Great player. A lovely bloke, as well. Always encouraging you." Tommy Powell, too, always had time for younger players.

He saw the last match the Rams played before the war. Derby County 1 Aston Villa 0. He stood in the boys' pen. Jack Nicholas scored a penalty. War was declared the following day.

He first played for Derby County in 1941. He was at a youth club on the Firs Estate on Christmas Eve when in strode the Rams stand-in manager Jack Nicholas. "You're playing in the first team tomorrow," he said to Tommy. "Jimmy Hagan can't get. You'd better get off home." The match was played on Christmas Day morning, against an RAF Select XI, and 10,000 people turned up to watch. Tommy Powell was 16 years old.

In 1942 he signed professional. The signing-on fee was £10. "Don't tell the tax man," he'd say years later. He retired in 1962 and was one of the few players to be honoured by the Football League for a career of over 20 years. He was proud of that achievement and the statuette he received.

He never sought recognition off the field and always lived within walking distance of the Baseball Ground. One Saturday he was walking to an FA Cup-tie against Northampton Town. The gate was 38,000, a record at the time. As Tommy walked along Cambridge Street, a chap ran towards him. "You'll never get in, mate," he shouted, "they've locked the gates."

On the field, Tommy Powell was recognisable. In black and white, a pale, slightly stooping figure, with immaculate ball control and superb passing ability – and his 'pull the ball down' trademark. How beautifully he did that, in the shadow of the Offilers Ales stand, as the spray flew and the crowd swayed in anticipation of the heavy ball heading towards them. They needn't have worried and although his stamina wasn't enough to cope with the middle of the Baseball Ground pitch in December, come the spring and in the autumn, Tommy Powell's skill and ability charmed us all.

In 1956-57, as Derby scored 111 goals to win the Third Division North championship, Powell's supply of crosses to centre-forward Ray Straw helped Straw equal the club's individual scoring record for a season. For any Derby supporter now in their mid-50s or older, those were glorious, golden days. And Tommy Powell was one of the stars.

For many years, he and his wife Gladys were season ticket holders in 'B' Stand, until the move to Pride Park. But Tommy Powell never really left the Baseball Ground. Appropriately, before his funeral service in September 1998, at a packed church in Normanton, the hearse paused for a few minutes outside the ground and, later, his ashes were scattered on the pitch.

Jesse Pye – he had a few tricks

JESSE Pye had already made his name when he joined Derby County in October 1954. In fact he was well past his peak, being nearly 35 years old when he arrived at the Baseball Ground, but Rams' supporters have always been able to recognise a good footballer when they see one and Pye was high up in that category. Footballing centre-forwards were not always plentiful in an era in which wingers were expected to get down the touchline and put in centres to the far post. The battering ram, good-in-the-air type of centre-forward, like Nat Lofthouse and Bobby Smith, was still popular in the mid-1950s – and very effective – so someone like Pye, with his neat control, subtle skills and easy style was comparatively unusual, despite the presence of smaller footballing types like Charlie Wayman and Ronnie Allen and in between all-rounders, like Roy Swinbourne and Tommy Taylor.

Pye made his name with Wolverhampton Wanderers and was 19 years old when war broke out in 1939, another for whom the war took some of the best years. He did play at inside-right in a 'victory' international match for England against Belgium at Wembley in 1946, after which he was transferred from Notts County to Wolves and scored a hat-trick against Arsenal on his debut. He switched to centre-forward and in the 1949 FA Cup Final scored twice, one a running header in picture-book style, as Second Division Leicester City were beaten 3-1. He also won his only England cap in the same match, against the Republic of Ireland at Goodison Park, that Bert Mozley made his England debut. He played 188 League matches for Wolves, scoring 90 goals, before joining Luton Town in 1952.

Not only did Pye have good ball control, he had a few tricks. In those days youngsters were encouraged to display tricks in matches and not let them remain hidden on the training ground. Confident performers would produce crowd-pleasing moments and Pye's 'flutter of the foot over the ball' and 'drag back under the sole of the boot' were featured in most of the matches in which he played. In addition, he once had that priceless commodity of speed off the mark, which in his prime, enabled him to leave defenders trailing once he had sold them a dummy, or even two.

On the field he played so confidently, but off the field he suffered from a speech stammer. It didn't prevent him from having words of encouragement for younger players and his reputation with players at Derby was very high. Peter Newbery was a part-time professional at the time: "I remember with great affection Jesse Pye, who was not only a good player, but really a nice man as well and very encouraging. Very few of the pros were encouraging, so far as the youngsters were concerned. Whether they felt you were a threat to their places I really don't know, but Jesse was a great guy."

Derby County were relegated to the Third Division North in Pye's first season, but he scored 16 goals in 31 League appearances the following year. Time, though, was catching up and he made only a handful of appearances as the Rams swept to promotion the following year. He left to join Wisbech Town as player-manager in July 1957 and had a long association with them. Wisbech was just one of several quite wealthy non-League clubs who were able to offer attractive wages and, if necessary, find jobs for players leaving full-time football. The combined packages included housing and, in the days of the maximum wage, many players found themselves considerably better off financially.

Jesse Pye died in Blackpool in February 1984, aged 63.

Peter Ramage – never stopped running

SCOTSMAN Peter Ramage played in two Derby County teams that finished runners-up in the old Division One, in 1929-30 and 1935-36. In a ten-year period when Derby were often challenging for the championship, Ramage was a consistent, but often undervalued performer at inside-forward. Not by everyone. "He never stopped running, Peter," said left-winger Dally Duncan. "He always played a lot to his winger, both wingers, and he made a lot of goalscoring chances for me." Supporter George Beard saw him play throughout the 1930s: "Peter was brilliant. Not a great goalscorer though. He was a plier of passes, when we had what we don't have now – wingers."

Ramage was signed by George Jobey in 1928, from Coventry City, but didn't get a regular place until George Stephenson was transferred to Sheffield Wednesday in February 1931. Once established, Ramage didn't miss many matches and was instrumental in creating goals for more famous names like Jack Bowers, Hughie Gallagher, Charlie Napier, Sammy Crooks and Duncan. In all, he played 255 matches for Derby County and scored 60 goals. It was a useful ratio for someone who had a reputation not noted for goalscoring.

He wasn't universally appreciated on the terraces, but he was by his teammates. Said Sammy Crooks, "He was a great forager, a glutton for work and one of the best clubmen Derby have ever possessed. He was always there to help you out of trouble and had he been with a London club he would have been hailed as a second Alex James. His positional play and ball distribution were second to none."

Ramage's best-remembered moment came when he scored an extra-time winner, a header, against Sunderland in a sixth-round FA Cup replay in 1933. The attendance at Roker Park was a record 75,118, with thousands more locked outside. One man died in the crush after the gates were closed and another died during the match after Sunderland were disallowed a goal by Bobby Gurney for offside. Four trainloads of Derby supporters were turned back several miles from Sunderland when it became obvious they couldn't get to Roker Park in time and because of the crush inside the ground, the kick-off time was brought forward and the match started early.

Despite that dramatic occasion, Ramage's most indelible memory of playing for Derby County was a match against Aston Villa at Villa Park, when the Rams fielded an all-Scottish forward line. Sammy Crooks was injured and Jimmy Boyd made his debut on the right wing alongside Charlie Napier, Hughie Gallacher, Ramage and Duncan. Boyd and Gallacher scored in a 2-0 win for the Rams.

Ramage left Derby County in 1937 and joined Chesterfield where he played almost to the outbreak of war. After the war he played first for Atherstone Town and then, approaching his 40th birthday, for Ilkeston Town. Said Tommy Powell, "It was about 1942 when I signed and we started playing matches in a local league against local sides and that. The fellow who was in charge of us then was Peter Ramage. 'Cor!' I said to my uncle afterwards, 'I take it all back.' I said: 'He makes the ball talk. He never gives it you if you are in trouble.' I said, 'He's absolutely brilliant.' Dally Duncan always said to me, 'I wouldn't have got a cap without Peter Ramage.' That's praise and he was a lovely bloke as well."

Born in Bonnyrigg in March 1908, Peter Ramage died in Ballydlare in December 1982.

Fabrizio Ravanelli – all the credentials

DATELINE: 6 August 2001. It's a bit early to start talking about centre-forward Fabrizio Ravanelli as a Derby County legend – he only signed for the club last week – but it may happen. He follows a strong line. Jackie Whitehouse, Harry Bedford, Jack Bowers, Hughie Gallagher, Jackie Stamps, Ray Straw, Bill Curry, John O'Hare, Roger Davies, Bobby Davison all made their marks and were crowd favourites. What is not in question is that Ravanelli has all the credentials to join that band, including plenty of talent and a big personality. If he does provide the goals that are needed for Derby County to retain a place in the ever-demanding Premiership, supporters who have welcomed his arrival rapturously will have no doubts. It is a tough task for the flamboyant Italian, but whatever happens the signing doesn't lack imagination. It indicates the club's determination to retain its reputation within English football. Remember, Derby County were one of the 12 founder members of the Football League, way back in 1888.

Ravanelli did not have an easy entry into top-flight Italian football. He was nearly 24 years old when he signed for Turin giants Juventus in 1992. He'd already been a professional for six seasons, beginning his career at Perugia, his home-town club, in season 1986-87. Two years later he moved to Avellino, but was not successful and had a loan period at Casertana, in 1989-90. He was then transferred to Reggiana where he scored 24 goals in two seasons and that brought him to the notice of Juventus. Gianluca Vialli was leading scorer with 16 goals when Juventus won the Italian championship after a gap of nine years and Ravanelli scored 15 times. He also scored all five goals in a UEFA Cup victory over CSKA Sofia. In 1996, Juventus won the European Cup in Rome, beating Ajax 4-2 on penalties. Ravanelli scored the goal for Juventus in the 1-1 draw, which took the match to the deciding shoot-out. He has also played 22 times for Italy and scored on his debut in Salerno, against Estonia, who had Mart Poom in goal.

He signed for Middlesbrough in July 1996 and played 33 games in the Premiership the following season, scoring 16 goals, all but two coming at the Riverside Stadium, where he scored a hat-trick against Derby County in a 6-1 victory. Despite his efforts, Middlesbrough were relegated that season and were penalised three points for failing to turn up for a game at Blackburn, just before Christmas. They claimed they couldn't field a team due to injury and illness. Had they played the game, with any sort of team, Coventry City would have been relegated instead. Even so, the margin would have been slight and Middlesbrough had a poor League season anyway, which was not alleviated by reaching both the Coca-Cola and the FA Cup Finals.

Ravanelli voiced several controversial opinions whilst on Teeside, including criticism of Middlesbrough's training facilities and methods. Teammates and supporters were sometimes less than enamoured with him and it does seem that controversy is never far away with the 'White Feather'. He left Middlesbrough for Marseilles in September 1997, and scored 13 goals as Marseilles were runners-up in the French League. He then returned to Italy to be a squad player with Lazio as they won the League title under Sven-Goran Eriksson.

In many ways, Ravanelli is an English-type centre-forward who leads the attack in the traditional way. Very left-footed, he positions well and holds the ball up until support arrives. He is not blessed with great pace, but his strength and determination in the penalty area is impressive and besides a consistent scoring record, he seems to be a player with whom other players are able to play, but there are not many frills to Ravanelli, the player. Those wait until after he scores. Then the celebrations begin. Like Mick Channon's whirling arm and Denis Law's raised clenched fist, the 'shirt over the head' routine comes into play. Plenty have tried, but no-one in football does it quite like Fabrizio Ravanelli.

Bruce Rioch – no frills and powerful

POWERFUL is the word which best describes Bruce Rioch. Powerful shots; powerful tackles; powerful crossfield passes; powerful long strides; powerful personality. Rioch was essentially a no-frills player and must have been very intimidating to play against. He was also mightily effective and his contribution in midfield to Derby County's second championship triumph, in 1975, included 15 League goals. Several of those were spectacular efforts, with the ball hitting the net with irresistible force. He would certainly have had some fun with the modern ball, which flies faster and swings about more than those used in the 1970s. That potent left foot would have warmed the fingers of a few Premiership goalkeepers, despite the gloves they wear. One thing you could be sure of was that when Rioch lined up a shot from 20 yards, spectators in the vicinity of the goal began to pay close attention.

He was signed for Derby County, by Dave Mackay, in February 1974, coming from Aston Villa where he had spent almost five years, but he started his professional career nearly five years earlier at Luton Town. At Luton, he often played as a striker alongside former Derby County centre-forward Ian Buxton, but by the time he arrived at the Baseball Ground he was a tall, well-built, mature and experienced midfield player of 27 years of age, three matches short of 300 League games and with 81 League goals under his belt. He played with an upright style, but he could be abrasive and some of his wilder tackles made strong men flinch. When seeking to correct a perceived injustice on the field, subtlety was not the Rioch way.

The Rams finished third in 1974, Rioch taking over the number-four shirt from the injured Henry Newton. That number was an indication of which side of the pitch he tended to play for Derby County. Surging in from the right, the angle was opened up for some ferocious left-foot shooting, but it didn't work out like that in the beginning. In 13 League appearances to the end of the 1974 season, Rioch netted only two goals and both were from the penalty spot. There was little indication of the scoring successes to come.

In both championship-winning seasons of 42 League matches, Derby County used a total of only 16 players. Goalkeeper Colin Boulton played throughout each campaign, but Rioch was the only outfield ever-present in 1975. He also played in every Cup match, a total of 54 matches for 20 goals. Whilst he was with Derby County, he played 18 times for Scotland and he captained his country in the 1978 World Cup finals in Argentina, although he was born in Aldershot. His father was a soldier and when Rioch later went into management, reporters were inclined to make a connection to explain his reputation as a disciplinarian.

Colin Murphy sold him to Everton in December 1976 and Tommy Docherty brought him back a year later, but it wasn't a happy ending the second time around. He eventually fell out with Docherty and Colin Addison and had spells on loan at Birmingham City and Sheffield United. After that he went to America to play for Seattle Sounders and, intriguingly, he combined that with being player-coach at Torquay United. Eventually he became manager at Torquay and later he managed Middlesbrough, Bolton Wanderers and Arsenal, where he signed Dennis Bergkamp. Unfortunately, his inability to suffer fools gladly didn't endear him to the London press and he gave way to Arsene Wenger. He has also had spells as manager at Norwich City and Wigan Athletic.

Reg Ryan – shrewd tactician

IN 1955, Derby County were preparing for life in the Third Division North. The plunge to the lowest division from the higher echelons of the First Division had been quite unexpected for supporters still savouring the 1946 FA Cup triumph and the record-breaking transfer deals of the late 1940s. In the decades immediately prior to and after World War Two, Derby County was one of the elite clubs in the country, but now the Rams were competing, for the very first time, with clubs like Accrington Stanley, Gateshead, Southport, Workington, Barrow and Chester, none of which survives in League football today. Yet the first match in the Third Division North produced an attendance of 24,169 at the Baseball Ground, for the visit of Mansfield Town. More remarkable still, the kick-off was delayed until the Saturday evening to avoid losing spectators to a Derbyshire cricket match that afternoon.

The average for the season was 17,704 as the Rams finished second in the table, to Grimsby Town. Only one promotion place was available, so they had to try again the following season when the Baseball Ground League average attendance rose to 19,609, with a top figure of 29,886 – and Derby County won promotion. Moreover they did it by playing attractive, attacking football and scoring lots of goals. Over 100 goals were scored in each of two seasons and supporters loved it.

Supporters old enough to remember those days always pay tribute to the part played by Reg Ryan. 'Paddy' Ryan was born in Dublin and was signed by Harry Storer from West Bromwich Albion in the 1955 close season. Significantly, it was Storer's first signing and the manager wanted Ryan as much for his leadership qualities as for his midfield schemer's role. Storer was well aware that Ryan was a shrewd tactician. He'd been at The Hawthorns since 1945 and was approaching the end of his career when he arrived at the Baseball Ground, but he was an established Irish international and was in the West Bromwich Albion team that almost did the double, for the first time in the 20th century, in 1954. They won the FA Cup by beating Preston North End 3-2 and finished runners-up to League champions Wolverhampton Wanderers.

In three seasons at Derby, Ryan missed only three matches. He made 139 appearances and his keen positional sense and accurate passing knitted things together in midfield, in the hurly-burly of the Third Division. During his early days at Derby, he used to travel daily to training with Storer, from Coventry, where they both lived. In an era when managers stayed mostly in the office and didn't appear too often at the training ground, the captain was an important link between players and 'the boss'. Trainers did the training and managers recruited players who, in Storer's words, 'could play' and they were expected to get on and do so. They were expected to work things out on the field for themselves and formal tactical talks tended to be few and far between. A word in a player's ear before kick-off and at half-time was the traditional approach of the manager who kept his overcoat on.

That's not to say everything was unplanned. Patterns and styles of play were usually laid down in pre-season. 'Push and run' at Tottenham, 'longer ball' at Wolves and woe betide anyone who forget what he was supposed be doing at Molineux, under Stan Cullis' eagle eye. No doubt the talks between Storer and Ryan, in the car on those daily journeys to the Baseball Ground, had much to do with Derby County's success in that period. Ryan himself used to say, "I signed for the manager, not the club, when I came to Derby."

He left for Coventry City in September 1958 and later worked for West Bromwich Albion as a scout. He was a familiar and popular figure at League grounds in the Midlands, especially the Baseball Ground, and until his death was a keen supporter of the Derby County Former Players Association. On attending his first dinner he walked in to see Tommy Powell, Dennis Woodhead, Terry Webster and Glyn Davies, all members of the Third Division North side, chatting. His eyes lit up: "Ah, the Northern team!"

Dean Saunders – balance, agility, fitness

DEAN Saunders was signed by Arthur Cox from Oxford United in October 1988. Peter Shilton had been signed in June 1987, Mark Wright in September that year. They were all a part of Robert Maxwell's master plan to lead Derby County on to great things. Instead, the master plan eventually led to relegation. From a position of fifth in Division One in 1988-89, Derby fell to 16th the following year. At the start of season 1990-91, Maxwell announced that the club was up for sale; at the end of season Derby County were relegated. Maxwell blamed lack of support at the turnstiles and also 'the local media conducting its long standing vendetta against the club and those who run it'. BBC Radio Derby commentator Graham Richards was banned from the ground, joining Lionel Pickering on the sidelines. Pickering had earlier been banned for going public about his offer to buy the club from Maxwell, an offer which was rejected.

Throughout the turmoil, Saunders played on. In that relegation season he made 38 League appearances and scored 17 goals – nearly half of Derby County's total tally of 37. It was an outstanding achievement, recognised by Saunders being voted Rams Player of the Year for 1990-91. To enable the club to pay off Maxwell, Saunders and Wright, were sold to Liverpool in the close season – Saunders for £2.8 million – and Derby County began life again, in Division Two.

When Saunders started his career at Swansea Town, he played and looked like a poor man's Kevin Keegan. The perm, the build, the darting scuttling run, the eye for a chance in the penalty area, the enthusiasm, were all reminiscent of Keegan. Of course, Saunders was no Keegan, but he did go on to build an impressive career in his own right. Like it was for Keegan, though, it was a struggle at the start. He was first loaned out to Cardiff City and was then given a free transfer by Swansea. He joined Brighton and Hove Albion and from there he was sold to Oxford United for £60,000. He blossomed at Oxford and Cox paid £1 million to bring him to the Baseball Ground. Maxwell also owned Oxford and for some people it was simply a case of him switching money from pocket to another.

Saunders played in 144 League games for Derby County and scored 59 goals, some spectacular, and is one of only 12 Derby County players to have scored two goals on their debut. He raised expectations and spectators always knew that a goal was possible when Saunders was around. He was around often, as he was seldom injured, a tribute to his fitness, balance, agility and quickness. Perhaps most of all, supporters remember Saunders for his all-too-brief partnership with Paul Goddard. That short period brought a quality of football that reminded people of the championship teams.

At Anfield, Saunders never seemed comfortable, never looked like a Liverpool player. He moved to Aston Villa a year later, in 1999. Three seasons at Villa Park, then it was off to Turkey and Galatasaray and, after a year, back to Nottingham Forest. Then it was on to Benfica in Portugal before the wanderer returned to Bradford City, a forward playing in the Premiership at 37 years of age. He won 15 caps for Wales while he was at Derby County and now has 73 international caps in his locker. He needs one more international appearance to take him into second place in the Welsh all-time list, ahead of Ian Rush and Peter Nicholas Don't bet against him making it.

Peter Shilton – mistakes were so rare

'GOALKEEPERS are like good wine, they mature with age.' Whoever said that could be right, but many people thought that Peter Shilton was past his best when he joined Derby County from Southampton in the close season of 1987. This, after all, was a man who had already won a League championship medal and two European Cup winners' medals with Nottingham Forest; who had 91 England caps to his name, had played nearly 800 League matches in his professional career.

That professional career began in the year after England won the World Cup in 1966. In fact, he'd played for Leicester City, as a 16-year-old amateur, the year before. It all meant that Shilton was within a month or so of his 38th birthday by the time he arrived at the Baseball Ground. It's an age when most professional players – goalkeepers, or otherwise – have hung up their boots, or gloves. Not Shilton. He went on... and on... and on, to become not only Derby County's oldest debutant, but also the club's oldest-ever player. In his final match, Shilton was aged 42 years and 164 days. Not even Steve Bloomer could match that. Shilton was a phenomenon if only for his longevity, but he could also keep goal. He accumulated another 34 England caps whilst he was with the Rams. Passed his best? Possibly, but even so, many good judges reckon Shilton was the best goalkeeper Derby County has ever had.

Goalkeepers born, not made. Really? Shilton wasn't a 'natural' goalkeeper. Not like Ray Clemence, who seemed more to epitomise the athletic build and soft hands that goalkeepers need. Shilton, with his burly frame and slightly old-fashioned look, wasn't like that. During his early career at international level, when Ron Greenwood was England manager, Shilton often found himself sitting on the bench whilst Clemence kept goal. Eventually, though, by dint of determination and application, Shilton made himself undisputedly the best. Not spectacular like Reg Matthews, not as flamboyant as Les Green, didn't command the penalty area as well as Mart Poom and what he'd have done with the back pass is problematical. Perhaps he was more like Colin Boulton, really. Safe, sure, steady, reliable, few mistakes and sometimes, inspirational.

Shilton was single-minded about goalkeeping and his training sessions were awesome in their intensity. He understood his own business better than anyone and wasn't interested in training that didn't suit him. It wasn't by accident that when pre-match warm-ups on the pitch became fashionable, Shilton never appeared. He preferred to do his own thing, in the dressing-room. What others did was their business. All this didn't mean that he wasn't a student of other goalkeepers and their methods, or didn't have some interesting thoughts about football itself, but long before specialist goalkeeping coaches arrived on the scene, Shilton understood that goalkeepers are a footballing race apart. They walk alone.

He made 211 appearances for the Rams. Of those, the match at Newcastle, in November 1987 was most memorable. Shilton saved everything. Persuading a Geordie crowd to applaud one of the opposition takes some doing, but on that day, St James's Park rose to him.

He had mannerism. He used to shake his head a little from side to side, when a shot went close. He clapped his hands, just in front of his knees, like a seal clapping for fish, to encourage those in front of him. Mainly, though, like good goalkeepers do, he seemed to fill the goal. More than any goalkeeper I've ever seen, he filled it, with massive authority.

And he kept on playing, until his last League appearance for Leyton Orient in January 1997, by which time he was 47 years and four months old and had taken his tally of appearances to a remarkable 1,005 in all.

Jim Smith – a great personality

JIM Smith was born in Sheffield and grew up on the Shiregreen council estate. He went to Harley Brook Junior School and although not many boys from Harley Brook passed the 11-plus exam to go to grammar school in those days, Smith did. It meant he went to Firth Park Grammar School, where he became captain of the school football team. He also learned to fight. He won the Sheffield boys' title at the second attempt and only lost on points in the final of the Yorkshire championships. In a manner of speaking, he's been fighting ever since.

Smith was a supporter of Sheffield Wednesday, a 'Wednesdayite', but it didn't prevent Smith joining Sheffield United as an amateur when Joe Mercer was manager. He didn't make the Sheffield United first team and moved to Aldershot in 1961. He joined Halifax Town in 1965 and Lincoln City in February 1968, where Graham Taylor and Ray Harford were playing colleagues. He was released at the end of the 1968-69 season and became player-manager of Boston United.

Smith values his time at Boston highly. They were a very prominent non-League outfit and Smith learned much about management there. There's no doubt that in the rush to appoint high profile managers from abroad, or top players into the manager's seat, the valuable apprenticeship served by men like Smith, at places like Boston, is being lost.

Smith was three years at Boston and then applied for the player-manager's job at Colchester United. He claims it's the only job he's ever applied for, which indicates how most appointments in football are made. They are made on insider knowledge, which is how, after a roundabout route via the manager's seat at Blackburn Rovers, Birmingham City, Oxford United, Queen's Park Rangers, Newcastle United, Middlesbrough (coach) and Portsmouth, Smith arrived at Derby County.

Smith had been sacked at Portsmouth and was missing the everyday involvement of football management. Then came the call. He says, "Well, the phone call wasn't quite in the middle of the night. At that time I was the chief executive of the Football League Managers' Association, living in Portsmouth, although we were on the point of moving back to Oxford. I had a phone call from a Graham Smith, who I know very well. Graham used to play for West Brom and Notts County, I think it was. I know I tried to get him to sign when I was at Boston. He'd been with Adidas and he's an agent, really and he asked me if I'd be interested in a chance to join Derby County. I think it was a contact through Stuart Webb, to be honest, via the board."

Gordon Hughes played at Lincoln City with Smith and was also a player with Boston United when Smith was player-manager. He's been a friend of Smith's ever since. Says Hughes, "It was funny. We travelled up to Wembley from Portsmouth. England were playing Japan that day and whether it was a coincidence or not, who was sitting next to Jim, but Stuart Webb. Whether it was coincidence, but they were having a natter and, probably, he was being sounded out then. So I had an inkling and I knew Jim would take the Derby job if it were offered – no doubt about it. And what a wonderful job he's done."

Smith has been manager at Derby County longer than at any other club he's been at. He says it will be his last job in management. His achievements over the years are a matter of record, but that says little about the man himself. Perhaps Gordon Hughes is best placed to comment on Jim Smith's approach of taking his business seriously, but of not taking himself too seriously in it: "You could write a book on Jim's office. You could interview the Allisons, the Fergusons, whoever you would want to say, the top managers in the game, and they're all roaring and laughing with Jim. He's a great personality. You could write a book on Jim's office, the people there... At times, the staff of say Arsenal, or Manchester United, have come in: 'Come on boss, we've got to move.' And they just can't leave Jim's office, you see. The tales that I've heard and they've all let their hair down when the adreneline is just coming down after the game. Wonderful. Wonderful conversation, if you're a sportsman, football. Tremendous. Of course, there's things you'd never dream of repeating. Honestly, Jim Smith has enlightened my life over the last 20 years and, yes, privileged is the word. He's a tremendous lad, a tremendous human being, which is really the most important thing, isn't it?"

Jack Stamps – a lion of a man

THERE'S a pub in the Market Place in Derby called 'Jack Stamps'. In 2001 there are plans to turn it into an Australian 'walkabout bar'. I'm not sure what Stamps would have made of an Australian walkabout bar in the middle of Derby, although he knew what a pint of beer was. Either way, to be recognised in such an overt manner, more than 40 years after you have retired from playing, says something about the place Stamps holds in the affections of the Derby footballing public. Some players just appeal to the imagination and Stamps was one of those.

What that means is that people like me, who never saw him play, have in their mind's eye an image built up through looking at photographs, reading material, seeing a few bits of film from old cinema newsreels, listening to recollections of playing colleagues and sifting valid opinions of people who did see him play. Like a jigsaw puzzle, the pieces of evidence collected fit together to produce a picture of a big, broad, bustling centre-forward, in a baggy white shirt and long black shorts, ploughing through the Baseball Ground mud in great big brown boots, towards goal. "A big bustler," said Jimmy Bullions. That's the image I have of him and when I talked to him in later years, he said nothing to alter that impression. Centre-halves must have known they were in for a serious game when Jack Stamps was around.

He was born near Rotherham and when he was given a free transfer by Mansfield Town, he joined New Brighton, who were in the Third Division North. Derby County manager George Jobey, who was always on the lookout for centre-forwards, signed him for £1,500 in 1939. He played against Aston Villa the day before war was declared and then the 20-year-old Stamps' best footballing years were taken away. He enlisted in the Royal Artillery and was one of the last members of the British Expeditionary Force to be evacuated from Dunkirk in 1940, during which time he was wounded. He then severed a knee ligament whilst playing in an Army match and it was thought his career was over. The knee did trouble him periodically afterwards, but it was 15 years later before he retired, with that 1946 FA Cup winners' medal.

Yet he might well not have played in the Cup run at all. When he returned after the war, he found Angus Morrison was occupying the number- nine position and Raich Carter and Peter Doherty were the inside-forwards. Luck then intervened... Dally Duncan was injured and Morrison moved to outside-left. Stamps then took over at centre-forward for the first-round tie against Luton. Duncan returned and Morrison went back to centre-forward for the first-leg of the next round, against West Bromwich Albion. For the second-leg at The Hawthorns, Stamps replaced the injured Doherty at inside-left, and scored a penalty. Doherty resumed against Brighton and Hove Albion who were the next opponents, and Morrison stayed at centre-forward. Things looked bleak for Stamps. Aston Villa were the opponents in the quarter-final, Stamps was recalled, the rest is history. Two goals in the Final at Wembley and the volley that burst the ball. That shot was on target too.

It must have been a great disappointment for Morrison to miss out, but in 1948 he was transferred to Preston North End. His FA Cup luck changed and he scored in the Final of 1954, when Preston beat West Bromwich Albion 3-2. Stamps went to help Sammy Crooks establish Shrewsbury Town as a Football League club and then served Burton Albion in a variety of capacities, but his eyesight began to fail and, for the last 20 years of his life, he was totally blind. He remained unfailingly cheerful, a big bear of a man with a huge paw which enveloped your hand and reminded you of his strength. The blindness didn't prevent him attending Derby County matches either, where his friend Maurice Hodgkin, himself a former Burton Albion player, acted as his eyes. In 1983 Jack Stamps became an honorary vice-president of Derby County. When he died in November 1991 the entire Derby County team attended his funeral at Winshill.

Billy Steel – you couldn't play with him

IT'S safe to say that Billy Steel wasn't the most popular player to pull on a Derby County shirt. At half-time in a match at Blackpool, Jack Howe threatened to hang him on a dressing-room peg and Howe was strong enough to do it. "Billy only played when Billy felt like it," said Tim Ward, who was not at all mean-spirited, but Ward wasn't the only player around who felt that Steel was not a good influence at Derby. Reg Harrison: "Good on the ball, but as Frank Broome once said, 'I get that ball and the only ball I can give is back to Billy Steel.' I never thought he was very good for the club, his attitude. Sometimes he wouldn't play." Johnny Morris: "Well, he was a typical Scottish player. Yes, a dribbler. He used to run himself into the ground. He was the type of player you can't play with."

No-one disputed that Steel had talent. Blond, 5ft 6ins, quick off the mark and with a body swerve to dream of, it was sometimes said that he could beat a man without even touching the ball. Perhaps he could, but colleagues were not quite so impressed. Some had played with Raich Carter and Peter Doherty, Sammy Crooks and Dally Duncan. They were hard acts to follow and they had consistency on their side, too. Steel, like many runners with the ball, blew hot and cold.

Off the field there were problems. Money he received from newspaper articles, his new car and his perceived 'star' status, they all unsettled players unused to such things. It caused resentment. Neither did it help that some of his off-the-field earnings were connected to chairman Oswald Jackson's business interests. Raich Carter, for one, wasn't pleased. Tim Ward again: "It didn't affect me in that way – I was just pleased to be back from a war where I'd seen friends killed – but I can quite see Raich's point of view. He was a great player, probably one of the greatest ever, and then Billy appeared on the scene, suddenly writing articles for newspapers and getting paid for it, driving about in a new car and all those sorts of things. In those days, people didn't go in cars. They were lucky if they got a lift off someone in a car. But Billy got everything."

Steel had a dark side to him too. Frank Broome recalled two of Steel's brothers-in-law calling at his club house in Hillsway, Littleover, 'looking for Billy, to sort him out'.

Derby County had broken the British transfer record to bring Steel to the Baseball Ground. The fee was £15,500 and was paid to Greenock Morton shortly after Steel had starred for Great Britain versus the Rest of Europe XI at Hampden Park. There was even some controversy before that match when Steel was chosen at inside-forward to partner Wilf Mannion, in preference to Carter. Steel played one full season with Carter, a total of 32 matches. In that 1947-48 season, Derby County finished fourth in Division One and were beaten in the FA Cup semi-final, by eventual winners Manchester United. It hardly represented failure, but the regulars still remembered Carter and Doherty. It was apparent that Steel couldn't really win.

He played, altogether, for three seasons at Derby County, making 124 appearances and scoring 35 goals. He also made 14 appearances for Scotland during that period. In partnership with Johnny Morris, himself another British record signing, he played 44 matches, but again the comparisons with Carter and Doherty were always present and, in September 1950, Steel returned home to Scotland. Dundee paid a record Scottish transfer fee of £23,000 for his services. His wife's illness and inability to settle in Derby was cited as being partly responsible, for which in the second half of the previous season he had received special permission to live in Scotland and train with Rangers. He enjoyed that, but when he attempted to extend the arrangement permanently, the Derby County directors refused. He emigrated to America in 1954, to play for Los Angeles Danes and he died in Los Angeles in 1984, aged 59.

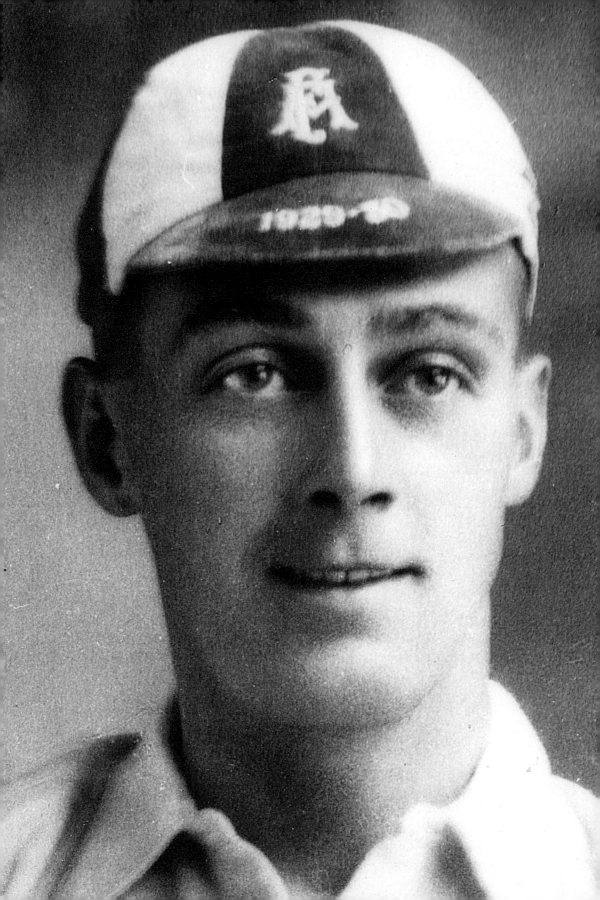

George Stephenson – neat and clever

GEORGE Stephenson played 120 matches for Derby County between 1927-30 and scored 56 goals, including four in a match against Grimsby Town. He also played twice for England against France, scoring twice, and Belgium in that period, but somehow, he is one of Derby County's 'forgotten' men. His brother Clem Stephenson, was much more famous. He was captain of the Huddersfield Town team which won the first-ever League championship treble in successive seasons 1923-24; 24-25; 25-26. Herbert Chapman was the manager for the first two title success, but he then left to manage Arsenal. The Arsenal team Chapman built dominated English football in the 1930s, emulating Huddersfield by winning a treble of championships, but Chapman died suddenly from pneumonia, in January 1934 and didn't see the second two title successes.

George Stephenson's link with Chapman was through Leeds City. Stephenson played for Leeds during World War One, when Chapman was the club's manager. On 4 October 1919, Leeds City were expelled from the Football League for making 'irregular' payments to players during the war years. Four directors and Chapman were banned for life, but Chapman appealed against the ban on the grounds that he was away working at an ammunitions factory when the illegal payments were made. He was reprieved. Leeds United were formed after the demise of Leeds City and were elected to the Football League in place of Lincoln City, who finished second bottom of the Second Division. They took over Leeds City's ground at Elland Road.

All the Leeds City players were put up for auction at the Metropole Hotel on 17 October 1919. Stephenson was sold by this method to Aston Villa, for £250, where he joined his two elder brothers, Jimmy and Clem. They never played together in the first team and shortly after George arrived at Villa Park, Clem left to join Chapman at Huddersfield. In 1927, George Jobey signed George Stephenson for Derby County.

A neat and clever inside-forward, Stephenson was a regular first-team player in his four seasons at Derby and it was something of a shock when he and centre-half Tommy Davison were suddenly sold to Sheffield Wednesday in February 1931. The Stephenson transfer actually went through in just over an hour, which indicates how little say players had in such matters in those times. Stephenson won another international cap at Hillsborough and later won promotions with Preston North End and was a member of the Charlton Athletic team that gained promotion from the Third Division South to the First Division in successive seasons. Like his brother Clem, he became manager of Huddersfield Town, but without success. He returned to Derby in the early 1960s, to look after the Derby County 'A' team, which played in the Central Alliance. His son, Bob, became one of only five players since the war to play football for Derby County and cricket for Derbyshire, although his career at both clubs was brief, making 14 and nine appearances respectively. He enjoyed greater success as a wicketkeeper for Hampshire, where he played for 12 seasons and eventually became Hampshire's captain.

Igor Stimac – he lit the spark

"STIMAC'S the name, Igor Stimac." No, he didn't introduce himself like James Bond, but no-one would have been surprised had he done so. Whatever 'presence' is, Stimac has it and his coming to Derby County a few weeks into the 1995-96 season had a similar effect on supporters as when charismatic figures like Kevin Hector, Brian Clough and Dave Mackay arrived at the Baseball Ground. The circumstances, though, were different. Dave Mackay was already an all-time 'great' when he signed for Derby County; Brian Clough was a name people knew about because of his goalscoring exploits with Middlesbrough and Sunderland; Kevin Hector was someone of whom football followers were aware. The difference was that no-one in Derby had ever heard of Igor Stimac. They soon did. Suddenly, the streets on the way to the match were dotted with supporters wearing the red and white chequered shirts of the Croatian national team, the name Stimac emblazoned on the back.

It didn't look very promising at first. A wet November afternoon in Tranmere and Derby County in the lower reaches of the 'new' First Division. Stimac scored after a corner – and the Rams lost 5-1. They slipped to 17th in the table. "It was a real shock for me," said Stimac, a year later. "I wasn't so frustrated after the game. I was thinking of the next game, because the next game was my first game before the Derby crowd at home, so it was a most important game for me. The Tranmere game was a really big shock, because we lost 5-1. It was the biggest defeat of the season, but I did score the goal." Then a flash of the confident Stimac: "I didn't play so badly, no?"

Had he wondered what he had let himself in for, I asked. "It depends on the character of the player," he replied. "I think that I am a strong character. I am always confident enough."

Why had he come to Derby, I wondered. Impatience surfaced: "Why, why? Lots of people used to ask me why, why? It just happened. It seemed like a good idea at the time. I was playing at that time in Croatia and I wanted to go abroad to play football. My agents were in contact with a couple of clubs and Derby was one of the clubs who was in a hurry to sign a new player and so I came here."

Amazingly, Derby County gained promotion at the end of that 1995-96 season. Many contributed, but it was Stimac who lit the spark. After Tranmere, the Rams won ten of the next 11 games. Stimac's class and leadership qualities shone through like a beacon and soon the chants of 'Igor, Igor,' began to ring around the Baseball Ground. When they did, Stimac responded like a knight in the Middle Ages acknowledging his sovereign. He'd turn and bow in return, in imperious style. Showmanship? Certainly. Supporters loved it and Stimac rapidly assumed cult status. His reading of the game, his calmness in possession, his air of authority – don't forget his physical strength – produced performances some of which were majestic. The Rams steamed into the Premiership on the back of an unbeaten run of 20 games.

Sadly, it all ended in tears. A clash of wills, perhaps? There was also a thought that Stimac was messing the club about and wasn't playing enough games, although in characteristic style, he pointed out that most of the games he did play in, Derby County won. Could the problems have been overcome with a little more sensitive handling on all sides? Who knows? What Stimac always appreciated was the city, its people and the supporters, but it was not to be. The relationship soured and in 1999, after 84 League appearances for the Rams, Igor Stimac left Derby County to join West Ham United. He went, owing nothing.

Harry Storer – a spade was a shovel

THROUGHOUT the 20th century ten players played football for Derby County and cricket for Derbyshire. Like Stuart McMillan earlier, Harry Storer went one better; he managed Derby County as well. He also played twice for England at football and was close to doing so at cricket and, uniquely, he was a football manager – at Coventry City – whilst still being a first-class cricketer. His father, Harry senior, also played for Derbyshire and was Liverpool's goalkeeper in the 1890s, and his Uncle William played cricket for Derbyshire, six times for England and also played football for Derby County.

Harry junior was brought up at Holloway, near Crich, but joined the Rams from Grimsby Town in March 1921, for £4,500. He played 274 matches for Derby County in the 1920s, being a member of the side which won promotion to Division One in 1925-26. In 1923-24 he had twice scored four in a single League game, against Bristol City when the Rams won 8-0, and in a 6-0 win over Nelson. He scored 24 goals that season, yet it was the only season he played in the forward line, really; Storer was first and foremost a hard-tackling wing-half.

He was a member of Derbyshire's only County Cricket Championship-winning team of 1936 and altogether scored 13,513 runs for the county, with 18 centuries, and also took over 200 wickets. So there wasn't much about football and cricket – and many other subjects, too – that Harry Storer didn't know. What he didn't know, he probably made up anyway. To say that Harry Storer was 'a character from a sporting family' is rather an understatement.

In the early 1950s Derby County fell swiftly from Division One to the Third Division North. Storer had been out of the game since leaving Coventry City and when he was appointed manager of Derby in July 1955 he first had to negotiate his release from a contract to coach cricket to campers at a Clacton holiday camp.

Storer was an immediate success as manager at the Baseball Ground, leading Derby County to promotion from the Third Division North in 1956-57. Some older supporters remember those days with great affection, as in successive seasons the Rams scored over 100 League goals and the crowds returned. Unfortunately, Storer couldn't maintain the momentum in the Second Division, despite some promising periods, and he resigned in 1962 to be replaced by Tim Ward.

The stories about Harry Storer are copious, some apocryphal. What is certain is that Storer was belligerent and blunt, often to the point of calling a spade a shovel. He had a jaw line like Desperate Dan and liked defenders who could tackle, hard. He preferred things simple. "Can he play?" was his inevitable question, after someone's detailed analysis of a player's technical ability. Coaching, he had little time for, although when he whispered a little homily in your ear at half-time, you hardly noticed the difference. He didn't go in for team talks much and rarely went to the training ground at Sinfin Lane. When he did, you knew there was trouble brewing. He had an answer for most things and when, on away trips, he settled down in the corner of your carriage on the train – 6.33pm return from St Pancras is ingrained in the memory – you knew the time would fly. Storer had a vast store of knowledge and he liked a good discussion, especially about how to play off-spinners on a turning wicket.

He also had a very hairy dog, called Bill, a sort of husky. The breed was used by Belgian trawlermen as guard dogs, because of their fierceness – or so Storer told us! Bill used to lie at the bottom of the three steps that led into Storer's office. Many an individual, who went steaming up the corridor after being dropped from the team, suddenly had second thoughts. As the poor fellow was trying to negotiate Bill, at the same time as Storer was blasting him with a few home truths, he usually realised that perhaps another time would be better. Oh yes, Storer knew a thing or two and Brian Clough, amongst others, admired him greatly.

Ray Straw – local boy made good

RAY Straw was a miner from Ilkeston, who equalled Jack Bowers's scoring record for Derby County of 37 League goals in a season. Bowers established his record in season 1930-31 in the old First Division and in only 33 matches, whilst Straw's 37 goals came in the Third Division North promotion season of 1956-57 and were scored in 44 appearances. That doesn't make Straw's achievement any less meritorious. Styles of play have differed in different eras, but what has not changed is the size of the goal itself, so 37 goals equals 37 goals in anyone's language and Straw's contribution to Derby County's rise from one of their lowest points in their history cannot be underestimated. For many older supporters, those two seasons in the Third Division North provided some of the most entertaining football of all and Straw's contribution of 51 goals in 67 matches had much to do with it.

Straw joined Derby County from Ilkeston Town where he had played a few matches in the Central Alliance, which was the premier local league at the time. Prior to that he had played for Ilkeston Miners Welfare. After scoring nine goals in seven games for Ilkeston Town, the 18-year-old swiftly came to the attention of Derby County and signed for the Rams in October 1951, initially as a part-time professional. He played in the final match of that Division One campaign, at home against Chelsea in a 1-1 draw. The attendance was a miserly 8,582, the lowest of the season, as spectators showed their dissatisfaction at the Rams' fall from grace and previous glories. The team finished in 17th position. The following year they were relegated, with Straw making 15 League appearances and scoring four goals, mainly deputising for the injury-prone Jack Lee.

As Derby County slid into the Third Division North and Straw fulfilled National Service duties, he made only six appearances in two years and it wasn't until Harry Storer took over as manager in 1955-56 that Straw established himself in the first team. With wingers Tommy Powell and Dennis Woodhead providing the ammunition, Straw's heading ability came into its own as Derby County scored 110 and 111 goals in successive seasons, the second of which they secured promotion.

If Straw was looking forward to life in Division Two, he was in for a shock. He was injured on a close-season tour of Holland and when the season began, he was sold to Coventry City after playing only five games. Storer was of the opinion he was unlikely to succeed in the higher division and he joined Coventry in November 1957. Coventry were then in the Third Division South, before becoming one of the founder members of Division Four in 1958-59. It meant that Straw is one of the few players to play in all six divisions of the Football League and he helped Coventry to promotion in that season. He didn't lose the knack of scoring at Coventry and in 143 League appearances scored 79 goals.

Big, strong and awkward, 'Tuffy' Straw – he had a penchant for sweets, especially toffees ('Tuffy' is local dialect) – was good enough to score 148 goals in a total of 281 League appearances and was useful enough for Raich Carter to sign him for Mansfield Town in 1961. There, he played for a season until his retirement from first-class football in 1962. Then, he went home to Ilkeston, where he died in May 2001. A local boy who made good.

Peter Taylor – the straight man

THE question is: Did Peter Taylor go down to the training ground? Kevin Hector smiles: "No. Peter Taylor didn't go to the training ground, not to mean anything." Willie Carlin reacts in surprise: "Who? Peter Taylor? Well, he used to give us tips. The only training he knew was racehorses." Colin Lawrence pondered: "Peter used to wander down sometimes. Not a lot." So what exactly did Brian Clough's assistant do? In the dressing-room, for example? Gordon Guthrie analyses: "Brian would sometimes come in and just say a few words and go. Then, of course, Peter Taylor would take over. He would probably go round one or two. If Brian had slaughtered one or two, he'd pull them back up." Steve Powell assesses: "Taylor was more of a straight man really. Clough would come in and, maybe, give us a rollicking and then he'd [Taylor] sort of calm things down, but together, as a pair, they were obviously very successful."

It's hard to talk about Taylor without mentioning Clough. After all, as far as Derby County is concerned, they were the pair who began the golden years at the Baseball Ground and, for six and a half years, Rams supporters had never had it so good. They were very much a partnership, but it was one where each knew his place. Colin Lawrence: "He [Taylor] always held that Brian was number-one. He always held to that, even when they went into the offices at Forest. Peter had the smaller office." Roger Davies: "Did Brian have the last word? I think he did. Overall, when push came to shove, Brian was the one, but Peter was brilliant. To play for Brian Clough was absolutely brilliant. Him and Peter Taylor, together. Brilliant."

Taylor was born in Nottingham in 1928. He was on Nottingham Forest's books as an amateur before joining Coventry City in 1946. He made 90 appearances for Coventry before signing for Middlesbrough in 1955 and at Ayresome Park, he made 146 appearances. As a goalkeeper, Taylor was sound rather than spectacular, more Ken Oxford than Reg Matthews; more Colin Boulton than Mart Poom, but the most significant happening at Middlesbrough was that some of his appearances were in the same team as a goalscoring centre-forward called Clough.

In *Clough: The Autobiography*, Brian Clough says, 'At the time I was Middlesbrough's fifth-choice centre-forward. Taylor's first words to me made a big impression: "I don't know what is going on at this club. You are better than anybody here." That was Peter. That was him throughout the rest of his life – instant judgment, taking little or no time, as long as it was based on what he considered to be solid evidence. And never the use of six words when two would do. I was a wide-eyed innocent in comparison and remember asking him in that first conversation after training: "How do you know I'm better than that lot?" He said: "You put 'em in the net better than anybody else. I'm a goalkeeper, so I know." As Eric Morecombe used to say, there's no answer to that, and I was not going to argue. Taylor's words were the first recognition I'd ever had as a footballer.'

They became friends. "It was always what I would call a 'professional within the game' relationship," says Colin Lawrence. "Outside of football, there was no interest, no. They'd meet up occasionally, that's all. On holidays they might meet up, occasionally. Peter was always very good with the children, with Brian's children. He'd play for hours with young Nigel. He could always flick a coin and make it come out of the joints of his hand and say: 'What's that Nigel?' Nigel would look away and there would be a two-bob piece, or something. Very good, very good. A dry sense of humour, Peter had."

Alan Hinton: "They were both very different, but very much a partnership and it was particularly sad when they fell apart and a lot of anger came into it. In the end we're all going to die and, of course, Peter died far too young." Taylor died in Majorca, in 1990, aged 62. As Clough said in tribute: "I am not equipped to manage successfully without Peter Taylor. I am the shop window and he is the goods in the back."

He had returned to Derby as manager in his own right in November 1982, signed Bobby Davison, Paul Hooks and Paul Futcher, and staved off relegation with a 15-game unbeaten run. But when the Rams were heading for the drop again in April 1984, Taylor departed once more. It was a sad end to his Derby days.

George Thornewell – flying right winger

MANY people who live in Duffield will remember George Thornewell as the landlord of the White Hart public house on Derby Road. Not many will remember seeing him as a flying right winger playing for Derby County and later, Blackburn Rovers, where he won an FA Cup winners' medal against Huddersfield Town in 1928. Thornewell was an archtypal, dribbling winger, whose job it was to get down the outside of the opposing full-back and cross the ball for traditional bustling centre-forwards to head goals. He'd joined Blackburn after serving Derby County for eight years.

"I left school at 14 and became a Rolls-Royce apprentice. Then the war broke out and I joined the RAF which had just been formed from the Royal Flying Corps. I trained as a pilot, but the war ended before I saw any action, so I went back and finished my apprenticeship." Such experiences gave many players a confident and mature outlook, which was also replicated in the years after World War Two.

Thornewell signed part-time professional forms for Derby County in 1919. He was still working at Rolls-Royce, but on completing his apprenticeship, he became a full-time player. He was a member of the team that participated in the Midland Victory League, along with Wolverhampton Wanderers, Aston Villa and West Bromwich Albion, which was played in April 1919 as preparation for the resumption of League football in August. When League football began again, Thornewell was on the right wing for the first match, a 1-1 draw against Manchester United at the Baseball Ground. Thornewell was an ever-present in that first season. It was a struggle. The Rams finished 18th in the First Division and were relegated the following year. Five seasons in the Second Division was followed by promotion in 1925-26, under manager George Jobey. Thornewell was still an automatic choice. In total he made 295 appearances for Derby County and scored 26 goals. He also won four England caps, but Jobey had other plans for the right-wing position at Derby. Thornewell was sold to Blackburn Rovers in December 1927 and was replaced by Sammy Crooks.

It was a good move for all parties concerned. Blackburn won the FA Cup that season, 1927-28, by beating Huddersfield Town 3-1 at Wembley, and Thornewell had a large part to play in Blackburn's first-minute goal, although he might not have played at all. He broke a collar-bone in the fourth-round tie against Exeter City, but fortunately, recovered in time for the Final. It was an era when goals were plentiful. The 'stopper' centre-half had not yet emerged and defences were often undermanned. Just up the road from Blackburn, Everton's Dixie Dean set a new League record with 60 goals in the season, breaking the record eight minutes from the end of the season with what was his 40th-headed goal. It beat the previous record of 59, set the previous season by George Camsell of Middlesbrough. Those really were halcyon days for centre-forwards, in no small part due to service they received from wingers like George Thornewell.

Thornewell left Blackburn in 1929, to join Chesterfield, and helped them win the Third Division North title in 1930-31 before retiring from football. During his time as mine host of the White Hart, he was a prominent member of the Derby County Supporters' Association and a familiar figure at the Baseball Ground.

Colin Todd – style and panache

COLIN Todd was one of the best defenders ever to play for Derby County. Not only that, he was one of the most watchable. He made the job look so easy. Defending, by its very nature, is a destructive business, but few players who were as efficient as Todd, had his style and panache. One who did was the great Bobby Moore, and Todd was unfortunate that their careers overlapped, otherwise Todd would have surely won many more than his 27 international caps for England. He also played twice for the Football League, made 14 appearances for England at under-23 level and played for the England Youth team. He won two League championship medals with Derby County, missing only five games in total in those seasons, and there were not many honours in football that were not won by him. Yet he played for six clubs, which was unusual for such a fine defender.

He joined Derby County from Sunderland in February 1971, a record fee being paid for the defender in the same week that Rolls-Royce in Derby went bust. He was one of Brian Clough's sudden signings, but Clough knew his man. After a knee injury brought a premature end to Clough's career, he was for a time Sunderland's youth-team coach and Todd was a promising apprentice. Todd was in Sunderland's first team at 18 years of age and went on to make 170 League appearances for them and a reputation as one of the most promising defenders in the country. When Clough paid £170,000 for him, chairman Sam Longson was on holiday when the deal was done and Clough sent him a telegram afterwards. With Dave Mackay in residence, Todd played initially in midfield to replace the injured Terry Hennessey and then at right-back for a while.

Mackay retired at the end of that season and Todd was then united with Roy McFarland in central defence. Gordon Guthrie: "I can't ever remember them panicking. Even some great players do, but I can't recollect them panicking. I mean, you used to say: 'Toddy's done it now, he'll never get out of there.' But he did and he'd just roll it and Roy, with that left foot, it was like a snake." In that first championship season, supporters voted Todd the Rams Player of the Year.

The 1974-75 season was probably Todd's best at Derby. McFarland ruptured an achilles tendon in an international match at Wembley and Peter Daniel deputised for all but the last four matches. Derby County took their second championship title and Daniel played superbly to win the supporters' award that Todd had won in the first championship year. The professionals, however, chose Todd as their Professional Footballers' Association Player of the Year, which is really the highest accolade a player can receive. Says Gerald Mortimer of the *Derby Evening Telegraph*: "I think the best single season I've ever seen from a Derby player was Colin Todd in 1974-75, when Roy McFarland was injured for most of the season and Peter Daniel played next to him and did a splendid job, but Toddy was as near flawless that year as ever I'm likely to see. He just made the game so simple in that he took the ball off opposing players and gave it to one of his own players and that was it."

Todd was not tall for a central defender, but he was extremely strong, compact and determined. He didn't get injured very often either, a tribute to his good judgment and excellent timing in the tackle. He played 635 League matches in his career, 293 at Derby County and played for Jim Smith at Birmingham City and Oxford United. Quick? Oh, yes, he was quick. Too quick for most forwards and, like the great Billy Wright before him, like lightning on the turn. Most of all he was a good footballer, comfortable in possession, easy to play with, confident and assured. Certainly one of Derby County's all-time 'greats' and, now back at Derby as assistant manager.

Frank Upton – strong men flinched

WHEN people talk about 'hard' men in football, there can be few who were harder than Frank Upton. A 6ft 2ins raw-boned blacksmith from Northampton, some of Upton's tackling made strong men weep. Of his early days as a part-timer at the Baseball Ground he recalled, "I worked at Derby Loco. I worked in the blacksmith's shop there and I used to have to get up at five in the morning. I used to live at the hostel. Remember it? I lived there and used to have to get up at five, walk into town, catch a bus, go to work, come back – I used to leave work about half three – catch a bus straight down to the Baseball Ground and do my training. Yes, Tuesday and Thursday nights. I thoroughly enjoyed it. I was a bit shattered when I got home though."

Not surprisingly, he doesn't have too much time for some of the modern theories about rotation and resting players. Upton's idea of rotation was to kick a few midfield players around the Baseball Ground, whilst rest was something you didn't get when you played against him. Most opposition players knew it. Yet he could play well enough to attract the attention of Bill Shankly and had an unfortunate illness to his daughter not arisen at a time when Shankly was looking to recruit a strong midfielder, he would have joined Liverpool when the Shankly revolution was just gaining momentum. Tommy Smith – and Frank Upton? Makes you think.

Upton joined Derby County from Northampton Town in 1953, after only 17 appearances for the Cobblers. He played little in the Third Division North championship season, partly because he was doing National Service at the time, but he established himself in Division Two. For a time Derby County's defence included other notable hard men like Les Moore, Tony Conwell, Glyn Davies and either Ken Oxford or Reg Matthews in goal. If the goals-against column suffered, so did a few opposing forwards. Upton also fancied a shot at goal, although 18 goals in 272 appearances for Derby County was a small return for someone who struck the ball so powerfully. Some of his passes, too, were hot to handle and there was a degree of irony in his eventual nickname of 'Stroker'.

He left Derby County for Chelsea in August 1961 and his career took a new direction. In a few of his 74 matches for Chelsea he played at centre-forward and helped them to promotion in 1962-63 and to a League Cup victory in 1964-65. Tim Ward re-signed him for Derby County in 1965 and he had a brief spell at Notts County and Worcester City, before joining Workington Town, then in Division Four, as player-manger in 1968. Upton turned to coaching and a variety of clubs all over the world, too numerous to mention, have benefited from his knowledge and enthusiasm, but he has always kept his home in the Derby area and retained a keen interest in Derby County.

He remembers one match well. "I can honestly say I never went over the top to anyone, but I remember the Southampton game, I remember that, oh yes. The lad Huxford came over the top of the ball to Glyn Davies and ripped his thigh wide open just above the knee. And the first tackle after, I lost my head I suppose. I'd seen the state of Glyn's thigh. The ref spoke to me and I said, 'Fair enough, sorry ref.' You know, like we used to, apologise to referees. I settled down then. The last ten minutes, though, he happened to come for a ball, 50-50, just outside our box. He was going to do me. So I just went for the ball, strong like. I went straight through him and I won the ball, no problem, but they carried him off, didn't they? I'd done the ligaments in his knee, but I just went for the ball. He was saying what he was going to do when we went down there, to Southampton, but he never came anywhere near. When we went down there, we never saw him. He was quiet as a lamb."

Ian Buxton also remembers: "Huxford, that's him. Huxford did Glyn and Frank did Huxford and Huxford and Glyn ended up in hospital beds next to each other. Both with about 15 stitches up the thigh and Glyn had stitches in the inner muscle as well! I think it was called a draw!"

Robbie van der Laan – a great talker

WHEN Jim Smith was appointed manager of Derby County in the summer of 1995, he had some wheeling and dealing to do. One of his deals brought Robbie van der Laan to the Baseball Ground, from Port Vale, for a fee of £475,000. Smith knew he needed a leader on the field and, although van der Laan was not the most skilful player Smith ever signed, it's doubtful whether he ever signed a better man for the particular job to be done. Van der Laan was wholehearted, strong and committed and exuded the qualities of effort and enthusiasm that football club supporters respond to. In every match, even for someone in the remotest seat from the the back of the stand furthest from the pitch, it was clear that van der Laan was trying his best. Moreover, he enjoyed a physical game.

He also took his captaincy duties seriously. "I've always been a talker – probably a better talker than a player," said the man born in Schiedam in Holland, despite his Potteries accent. "It's important for a captain to go out on the pitch and put into practice what the manager has been preaching. I have always been a talker and I think that helped the other players. There aren't that many talkers in football these days so it can be an advantage in team selection – you might get the nod over another player in the same position." It's a shrewd observation from someone who never took his selection for granted.

His finest moment for Derby County came when he scored the winning goal in the match against Crystal Palace which took the Rams into the Premiership in April 1996. He was at the back post when a corner came in. He remembers it, although not particularly clearly: "I thought 'this is it!' I was unmarked, got my head to it and, luckily, it went in. Jim Smith named me Man of the Match, but I think it was just the goal that clinched it because I didn't play any better than any of the other lads."

In two seasons in the Premiership, van der Laan made made 25 appearances, of which four were as a substitute. Never the quickest of players, he found the extra pace at the top level difficult to cope with, whilst injuries also began to take their toll. By this time, Igor Stimac was team captain, although van der Laan remained as club captain, but he finally left for Barnsley at the end of the 1997-98 season, following the Yorkshire club's relegation from the Premiership.

What makes a good captain? It's hard to say, really. The ability to inspire those around you to play as well as they can is, perhaps, the main quality a good captain needs. A championship success, an FA Cup win, or a promotion does help, too. At a crucial stage of Derby County's history, van der Laan played a vital role. In the line of Derby County captains remembered – and there are many, many more, who have long been forgotten – Robbie van der Laan can take a very honourable place.

Paulo Wanchope – so unpredictable

'IT all started so innocuously. Collecting a ball just inside his own half, Wanchope set off from a wide right midfield position and headed diagonally towards the Stretford End. A total of 4,088 United supporters, looking down from the third deck of the massive North Stand and a dizzy height of 35 metres, were reasonably relaxed as Wanchope began to move. The 7,352 spectators sitting in the second tier, with 32 hospitality boxes in the rear, felt fairly comfortable as he made ground through midfield, but 14,000 more committed fans, seated on two levels in the lower tier and nearer to the action and with 55 hospitality boxes behind, began to stir uneasily, sensing danger, as the penalty area hove into sight.'

There are debuts and debuts and anyone and everyone, who has ever played professional football, can remember their own. Later, when they have become hardened old pros with cold eyes, they don't usually bother too much about the debuts of others. Such things pass like ships in the night and are easily forgotten. Not Paulo Wanchope's debut. Those supporters who were among the crowd of 55,243 at Old Trafford, on Saturday, 5 April 1997 saw something special.

Nobody knew who Wanchope was, other than he was from Costa Rica. Apparently he had another surname as well – Watson – so for a while, he was occasionally referred to as Wanchope-Watson. It was also rumoured he was a useful basketball player. That, we could believe. When he ran out at the so-called 'Theatre of Dreams' with his socks halfway down his calves – "We haven't got any socks long enough to fit him," said Jim Fearn, the Rams' press officer – the words that sprang to my mind certainly weren't 'suave' and 'sophisticated'. It looked more likely that the team bus had stopped along the way to pick up a straggler.

He was substituted after 65 minutes, as the Rams went on to record a memorable 3-2 victory. He didn't start in the next match either, at home to Southampton, to the dismay of supporters who'd witnessed the Old Trafford affair and, no doubt, had been talking about it ever since, and to the consternation of those who'd stayed at home and were now aching to see for themselves what all the fuss was about. Sometimes decisions made in football are short on horse sense.

Wanchope played two full seasons for Derby County, making 72 Premiership appearances plus seven as substitute. He scored 23 goals and Derby County finished ninth and eighth. He was tall, gangly, unpredictable, probably difficult to play with, certainly difficult to play against. He was extremely strong, he stayed fit, he worked hard, he worried the opposition and he played centre-forward. Off the field, in the dressing-room, who knows? With his contract due to run out at the end of season 1999-2000, he joined West Ham United for a fee of £3.5 million in July 1999, and later moved to Manchester City, with whom he was relegated from the Premiership.

'Such a long stride is devilishly deceptive. Philip Neville's legs were working overtime, but he was making no impression, as Wanchope loped on... and on. On he strode, to the edge of the United penalty area, brushing aside bemused defenders along the way with Neville still snapping away like a terrier at the heels of a Great Dane. Talking of which, out rushed Peter Schmeichel. He needn't have bothered. Wanchope, leaning left, very calmly slid the ball with his right foot past the goalkeeper's left-hand and watched it roll lazily into the back of the United net. The Stretfordenders were stunned as the ball nestled there, cosily, right in front of their astonished eyes. Amazing? I should say so. Disbelief floated around Old Trafford. Wanchope celebrated like a Harlem Globetrotter. Then, he was engulfed by delighted teammates'.

Note: The quoted passages at the beginning and end of this chapter are from the author's book *Journey Through a Season*.

Tim Ward – the gentleman footballer

TIM Ward's association with Derby County lasted over a period of 30 years. It was an eventful career. He was signed from Cheltenham Town in 1937; he was sacked as manager of Derby County in 1967. In between was the war in which he was slightly injured in the D-day landings. He missed out on the FA Cup Final in 1946, played twice for England in the early post-war seasons, toured Canada with an FA X1 in 1950, and surprisingly, was transferred to Barnsley on deadline day in 1951. He was informed at 6.30pm that Derby County had accepted an offer from Barnsley for his transfer. The transfer deadline was 10pm. His wife, Nancy. was out visiting friends. He signed at the Portland Hotel in Chesterfield. When Nancy returned, a neighbour informed her that he'd gone to sign for Chesterfield. Bewilderment all round.

After playing 33 League matches for Barnsley, during which he lived in a club house and paid £1 a week rent, he was appointed manager of Exeter City in 1953. He stayed only eight days, for one of the shortest-ever managerial reigns. Barnsley had retained his registration and he returned to Oakwell, aged 35, to become the youngest manager in the Football League. He moved to Grimsby Town in 1960, before arriving back at the Baseball Ground in 1962, to take over from Harry Storer. Eventually he was succeeded by Brian Clough, but not before he'd signed Kevin Hector.

Ward was a classy wing-half, who played 226 matches whilst he was with Derby County. "He was a gentleman footballer really," said Ray Young. Considering that those appearances were stretched over a period of 14 years, including the war, it is a tribute to his consistency that he missed only a total of 22 League matches in his career at Derby.

Ward made his debut in 1938 and remembered those days well: "I was really amazed when I came to Derby, at the discipline within the club. Young players, such as myself, the reserve-team players as well, were not allowed in the first-team dressing-room, except perhaps once a week to look at the team sheets on a Thursday afternoon. The first team were on a plane completely apart from everyone else. We looked up to the first-team players. They were gods. They walked up on the top of the mountain and we looked up to them and respected them and kept out hopes to ourselves that one day we would be able to walk with them."

Ward joined the army upon the outbreak of war in September 1939 and consequently made relatively few wartime appearances for Derby County. He did play against Luton Town in the first leg of the first tie of the 1946 FA Cup run, but was still not demobbed and was posted back to Germany where he was now serving with BAOR (British Army of the Rhine). He travelled home from there on the Wednesday before the Cup Final and as the Rams lifted the trophy, he watched from a seat in the stand. He took a philosophical view of missing the big day. "Some of my best friends were killed," he said. Once back, he regained his place in the Derby County team, which finished fourth in Division One in season 1947-48 and also reached the FA Cup semi-final. The following season they finished third, but by the time Ward left in 1951, the club was in decline.

Little money was available when he returned as manager. Derby County were an average Division Two side, but they did score goals. He paid small fees for Eddie Thomas and Alan Durban, who each scored 22 League goals in season 1964-65. Ron Webster became established, Ian Buxton prospered at centre-forward and young players like Phil Waller, Bobby Saxton, Mick Hopkinson and John Richardson were introduced. He signed Colin Boulton and Peter Daniel who, along with Durban, went on to greater glories, but his greatest legacy to the Clough and Taylor regime was Kevin Hector. He persuaded the directors to pay £40,000 for Hector. Later he complained: "I had to ask the directors' permission to stick a twopenny stamp on a letter."

Ward went to live at Barton-under-Needwood, where he spent many hours in retirement at the Dunstall Cricket Club's beautiful ground, which reflected his other great passion. He formed the ex-Rams X1 in the mid-1970s, which raised thousands of pounds for charity, and he was the first chairman of the Derby County Former Player's Association, formed in 1991. Tim Ward was held in such esteem that following his death in January 1993, a memorial service was held in Derby Cathedral.

Ben Warren – he always came home

BEN Warren played a total of 269 matches for Derby County between 1899-1907, of which 27 were FA Cup-ties. He played in the 1903 FA Cup Final when Bury beat Derby County 6-0, before a crowd of 63,102 at the Crystal Palace to record the biggest-ever victory in the Final of the competition. Steve Bloomer didn't play because of injury, and doubts surrounded goalkeeper Jack Fryer before the match. Fryer was injured, with the score at 2-0 and was replaced in goal by Charlie Morris. Fryer returned as a limping passenger only to eventually leave the field, but by that time the Rams were 5-0 down. Strangely, this was billed as a battle between two strong defences as Derby County had only conceded one goal on the way to the Final and Bury, none at all.

Much of Derby County's lack of success in the FA Cup – they lost three Finals between 1898 and 1903 and three semi-finals as well in the previous ten years – was put down to the 'gypsy's curse'. Legend had it that the club was being punished by a gypsy's curse when it moved to the Baseball Ground on the site of a Romany camp, in 1895. The following year, Derby County reached the semi-finals again, the seventh time in nine years. They lost again, 1-0, to Bolton Wanderers. It was claimed that only when the curse was lifted would Derby County win the Cup. One of the gypsies – Old Mallender – helped out on the ground, so who knows? Whatever, in 1946 an enterprising journalist took Derby skipper Jack Nicholas to a gypsy, a palm was crossed with silver – and lo and behold, Derby won the Cup.

Ben Warren was born in 1879, at Newhall, near Church Gresley and Swadlincote, in South Derbyshire. His first clubs were Newhall Town and Newhall Swifts before he signed for the Rams in May 1899, making his League debut in a 1-1 draw at Stoke in March 1900.

According to Jimmy Methven, who became Derby County's manager in 1906: "Benny Warren was one of the most wholehearted players who ever kicked a football and it was a wrench for us when we were obliged to transfer him, at his own request, from the County to Chelsea. As manager of the club I did my utmost to to persuade him to stay with Derby, but I failed."

Chelsea had only been elected to the Second Division in 1905-06, but they gained promotion to the First Division in 1907, replacing Derby County. Warren joined them the following year. It was thought that Warren soon regretted the move and he regularly returned, by train, to his Newhall home after Saturday matches in London.

He played 19 consecutive matches for England, 13 whilst with Derby County, and was recognised as one of the best wing-halves in the country. He also played at inside-forward and scored 33 goals for Derby. Eight of them came in the FA Cup in 1902, three of those in one game, against Lincoln City.

His life ended tragically. He retired from football in 1912, forced to give up the game following a bad knee injury, and Chelsea played a testimonial match for him. Soon after, he was certified insane and spent some time in the Derbyshire Lunatic Asylum. He died in Newhall in 1917. He was 38 years old.

Ron Webster – he knew his business

RON Webster played 17 seasons for Derby County and his total of 530 appearances, plus five as substitute, puts him second only to Kevin Hector in matches played for the club. In League matches only (451/4), he is in sixth place behind Hector, Jack Parry, Geoff Barrowcliffe, Steve Bloomer and Jimmy Methven. Of those appearances, less than a handful would be rated below par, for Webster was reliable, efficient and knew his business. He served under six different managers (although he never played a first-team game under Tommy Docherty) and was appreciated by each, which is testament to his consistency. Managers knew they could trust Ron Webster, whilst those who played in front of him soon realised that if they positioned properly, they would receive the ball early and at a decent pace.

Webster was born at Belper but played for Alfreton and District schoolboys. He used to go on the bus, with his dad, to watch Derby County play at the Baseball Ground in the Third Division North days. He would never have thought then that he was destined to win a League championship medal and play in the European Cup. He was the only local boy in Brian Clough's side of 1972 (discounting the very late appearance of the teenage Steve Powell).

He started out as a wing-half and it was reserve-team trainer Jack Bowers who first put in his mind the idea that he might be better at full- back. When Clough replaced Tim Ward as manager in 1967, it was to full- back that Webster went. He enjoyed it better. "I liked defending," he said. "I was a good defender. I filled the little gaps in and whatever."

Some people were inclined to underrate his ability and, perhaps, he did himself. "You know the wing-backs today? I don't think I'd be able to do that properly, you know, because I wouldn't be good enough when I got round their box. Round their box, I wasn't very good. I was good at getting it and giving it to players who could do it."

He makes it sound so simple, doesn't he? That, though, is the illusion, as many a winger found to his cost, for behind that apparently diffident outlook was the hard determination that drove a teenage Webster to walk into the lion's den of Harry Storer's office and put it firmly to one of football's fearsome characters that he, Ron Webster, should be given a chance in the first team, because he felt he could do the job better than the people who had been tried so far. Storer took him at his word. Webster never looked back.

Despite what he says, I think Webster would have coped just as well today. The athletic nature of modern football would not have bothered him. He could certainly run, smoothly and effortlessly, whilst ability is ability in any era. The better pitches, too, would have suited his essentially short-passing style, but most of all, he understood his own capabilities and disciplined himself to remain within them. It is true that professional footballers need to have talent and Webster was not short of that, but knowing how to use that talent is what real ability is about. Make no mistake, Ron Webster had real ability.

Jackie Whitehouse – inspiration to his colleagues

JACKIE Whitehouse was another in the long line of excellent inside-forwards, or centre-forwards, who played for Derby County between the two world wars. According to the *Derby County Supporters' Official Yearbook* (1962-63), the following words were written about Whitehouse at the end of his first season at Derby County in 1923-24. 'The influence which he has had upon the attack can hardly be measured. He has been worth every penny paid to Birmingham for him and is often an inspiration to his forward line colleagues.' That season Derby County were the most prolific scorers in the Second Division, with 86 goals. At the same time in the Second Division were Manchester United, Leeds United, Southampton, Leicester City and Sheffield Wednesday, together with Clapton Orient, Nelson and South Shields. Times do change.

Whitehouse scored 16 goals as Derby County finished third in the table and just missed promotion. In the last match of the season, at the Baseball Ground, the Rams needed to beat Leicester City 5-0 to pip Bury on goal-average for second place, behind champions Leeds United. The Rams led 3-0 at half-time and 4-0 after 65 minutes, but couldn't manage the final goal and promotion slipped away, by 0.015 of a goal. Whitehouse missed the last two games through injury and was thus robbed of an ever-present record. Had he played, then the Rams would probably have been promoted.

Although he joined Derby from Birmingham in May 1923, during World War One he had guested for the Rams and scored a few goals. Whitehouse was born in Smethwick in April 1897 and played in local football before joining Birmingham in 1916. In 1919-20 he scored seven goals in 36 games as the Blues finished third in Division Two. When they won the championship the following season, Whitehouse was a key figure with 11 goals in 33 games. But now the great Joe Bradford was becoming established and at the end of 1922-23, Birmingham let Whitehouse go.

In 1924-25 the Rams again finished third and again Whitehouse missed only two League games, this time scoring 13 of Derby's 71 League goals. Season 1925-26 marked a turning point for Derby County. George Jobey took over as manager from Cecil Potter and the Rams gained promotion. Whitehouse missed much of the second half of the season, recovering from appendicitis, and played only 19 League matches, although he still managed five goals. The following season, 1926-27, Whitehouse played 23 matches in Division One and scored 13 goals. Four of those came in one match at the Baseball Ground, against Sheffield Wednesday, when Derby won 8-0. The season after, 1927-28, Whitehouse scored 21 times in 37 League matches as Derby finished fourth and the club began to be a force in Division One.

The four goals Whitehouse scored in the drubbing of Wednesday were probably significant. By February 1929 he had played in 27 League games for Derby that season and scored 14 goals. He had enjoyed a prolific partnership alongside Harry Bedford, but now the Rams had another centre-forward, the young Jack Bowers, and Jobey felt able to let Whitehouse go. Wednesday must have remembered the four he put past them and he joined the Hillsborough club, coincidentally making his last appearance for Derby County against Wednesday. It was not a happy ending, however, the Rams losing 5-0. A foraging sort of player, Whitehouse made exactly 200 appearances for Derby County and scored 86 goals. Even in an era when goals were plentiful after the change to the offside law, it was a pretty useful record.

For Wednesday he played only ten games, scoring once, before moving to Bournemouth and then into non-League football. Jackie Whitehouse died in Halesowen in January 1948.

Geraint Williams – the powerful engine

'GEORGE' Williams was one of those underrated players who was more appreciated when he wasn't there than he was when he was! Signed by Arthur Cox from Bristol Rovers in March 1985 for £43,500 just before the transfer deadline, he played 330 games for Derby County, plus two as a substitute, which when added to around 150 appearances for Bristol Rovers, 217 for Ipswich Town and 40 for Colchester United, makes up a formidable appearances record. He wasn't 'not there' often and, although he may not have pleased all the critics on the terraces, he was certainly well thought of by those within the game and particularly those whose wages depended upon him.

Williams was not a streamlined express. He was more akin to those chunky, powerful engines that hauled heavily-loaded goods vehicles up and down the country in the age of steam. As they chugged backwards and forwards, delivering valuable items to important destinations, they were often overshadowed by their sleeker cousins flying along with splendid sounding names like *The Flying Scotsman* or *The Royal Scot*. They were the elite express trains, but the railway system also needs goods engines, just like all teams need a George Williams. He provided the balance between the artist and the artisan.

Never dismiss the artisan. He, too, is a craftsman and Williams brought a considerable number of assets to his midfield role. Good positioning, for one. He was invariably in the right place at the right time. Around his own goal for a vital interception. In the centre circle, with a jarring tackle. On the edge of the opposing penalty area? Oh dear... oh dear. When Williams fastened on to a loose clearance there, most supporters willed him to shoot. They knew that nobody in the side struck the ball more sweetly with his right foot, but if a Williams goal was rare, it was usually spectacular. The trouble was there weren't enough of them. It was as though Williams himself undervalued his shooting ability. The groans which greeted a safety-first sideways pass indicated what supporters thought. Ten goals in seven seasons showed they were right. Dribbling wasn't in the Williams repertoire either and sometimes his passing was erratic. On days like that he could be like the girl with the curl, very good, or horrid. Even on bad days, though, Williams didn't hide. Busy in the game was what he was about and always determined.

His midfield partnership with John Gregory was the fulcrum of Derby County's successive promotions from the Third Division to the First Division in the 1980s. During his years with the Rams he also won 11 caps for Wales. Two more came when he went to Ipswich. Never the most fluent of talkers to the press, he once gave a splendid interview for BBC Radio Derby, when he captained the side in a match at Portsmouth. Unfortunately, someone had neglected to put a tape in the recorder. It was Marco Gabbiadini's first match and he scored the only goal. Gabbiadini was left to take all the glory, as Williams, inadvertently, stayed in the background. Somehow, you felt he preferred it that way.

Kevin Wilson – managers valued him

THE word that springs to mind, when one thinks of Kevin Wilson, is brisk. Other words synonymous with brisk are sprightly, snappy, bright, lively, quick, active, nimble, zippy, alert, animated, buoyant. You get the picture? Wilson was all of these and, like Malcolm Christie, had an eagerness about his play which is often a characteristic of players who join League clubs from non-League outfits.

Wilson joined Derby County from Banbury United, in December 1979, as an 18-year-old centre-forward. He played 122 matches, plus 19 as substitute, and scored 41 goals for Derby County before moving to Ipswich Town, in 1985, for a fee of £150,000. The money was used by Arthur Cox, to acquire the transfers of Trevor Christie and Gary Micklewhite, whilst Wilson went on to play three seasons at Portman Road, making 98 League appearances and scoring 34 goals. He also became an Northern Ireland international – although his Midlands accent belies the heritage – and he went on to win 42 caps for Northern Ireland. After Ipswich came five years at Chelsea (41 League goals), where he was part of the promotion from Division Two, in 1988-89, followed by three years at Notts County, a brief loan to Bradford City and a four-year stay at Walsall. He then moved to Northampton Town as player-coach in 1998-99 and made eight more appearances in that season. He continued to be registered as a player at the Sixfields Stadium and was still making an occasional appearance as the 21st century arrived. It makes for a playing career of more than 21 years. Enthusiasm? That's Wilson.

Small for a striker, such players always tend to be measured against the yardstick of Jimmy Greaves. Wilson was no Greaves, but he was a neat, well-balanced player who scored some useful goals in a Derby County team that was heading steadily for the Third Division under Colin Addison, then John Newman and finally, Peter Taylor. It was also the period when director Stuart Webb was fighting to save the club from bankruptcy and it really looked as though the days of Derby County were numbered.

There were some high spots for Wilson at Derby. He played in the final match of Kevin Hector's illustrious career, against Watford at the Baseball Ground on the last Saturday of season 1981-82. Derby County needed a point to ensure survival in Division Two and Wilson missed a penalty early in the match, when he shot straight at goalkeeper Steve Sherwood. Fortunately for Wilson, he scored a deflected equaliser as the Rams pulled back from a goal down to win the match 3-2. Appropriately, the winner was scored by Hector, the 201st goal of his Derby County career.

Wilson ended the season as Derby County's leading scorer with nine League goals. He was a consistent player who managers valued, not least for the fact that he usually stayed fit, and his career tally of nearly 600 League matches is a remarkable achievement for a forward. He scored almost 150 League goals. Now manager of Northampton Town, he's probably still registering himself available to play, if selected.

Vic Woodley – retirement to a Cup Final

VIC Woodley arrived at Derby County just in time for the 1946 FA Cup Final. He was signed by manager Stuart McMillan, from Chelsea, less than two months before Derby played Charlton Athletic at Wembley. He owed his good fortune to the back and internal injuries sustained by regular goalkeeper Frank Boulton, in a collision with Trevor Ford, in a match against Swansea Town in February. Boulton had missed only three Derby County matches in the season before war broke out in 1939 and he continued to play, at various times, throughout the war years. In season 1945-46, when the Rams played in Football League South, Boulton resumed his duties as regular goalkeeper, but he'd never played at Wembley.

Woodley, on the other hand, was no stranger to Wembley. He'd won 19 England caps in consecutive matches in the immediate pre-war years, when he was in competition with such notable goalkeepers as Harry Hibbs of Birmingham City, Frank Moss of Arsenal and Ted Sager of Everton. He joined Chelsea in 1931 and made more than 250 appearances, but finally lost his place at Stamford Bridge and was playing in non-League football, for Bath City, when he received the call from Derby County, although Chelsea still held his registration.

Don Bilton was a Rams goalkeeper who had played a few matches during the war years. He took over from Boulton for a couple of matches, without looking convincing, so McMillan was forced to recall Billy Townsend, who was playing as a guest for Queen of the South. Townsend had a reputation for being nervous under pressure, but he came into the side for the sixth- round matches against Aston Villa on 2 and 9 March 1946 – up to the semi-final, matches were two-legged affairs. Townsend inspired little confidence. That prompted McMillan to act. Woodley was signed and made his debut in an away match against Coventry City on 14 March. A week later, he made his FA Cup debut in the semi-final against Birmingham, but it was in the replay where he distinguished himself by making a crucial save from Harold Bodle to keep the Rams in the game. Bodle was a goal poacher and when a Rams attack broke down on the edge of the Birmingham penalty area, Bodle was away on the counter-attack. It was a one-versus-one situation, but Woodley spread himself and deflected the ball with his legs for a corner.

Woodley then injured two fingers in an accident at work and the unfortunate Boulton returned to the team for a League South match against Luton Town, at the Baseball Ground. It wasn't a happy return. Boulton conceded three goals as the Rams won 4-3 and it was clear that Woodley would return. He did, for the hectic Easter programme of three matches in four days, a week before the Cup Final!

Remarkably, the combined attendances in the three FA Cup matches Woodley played in the process of winning his medal, was 243,622, an average of more than 80,000 spectators per match. The Cup Final was only his ninth game for the Rams and, in total, the 36-year-old Woodley played just 34 games for Derby County before returning to Bath City, as player-manager, at the end of the 1946-47 season. Sometimes, though, there's no substitute for experience.

Mark Wright – nothing he couldn't do

MARK Wright signed for Derby County for a fee of £760,000 in August 1987. A week earlier, Derby County had signed Peter Shilton, according to *The Mirror* newspaper, for £1 million. One each occasion, the selling club was Southampton and on each occasion the person who broadcast the news was new chairman Robert Maxwell. He loved publicity did Maxwell, preferably, his own. It was also Derby County's first season back in the old First Division.

Throughout his time at Derby, Wright, like all the playing staff, had to contend with the 'Maxwell factor'. In the early days of Maxwell's chairmanship, a banner used to be hung from the front of the Ley's Stand proclaiming, proverbially, that 'Robert Maxwell Walks on Water'. After all, wasn't this the man who had saved Derby County from going to the wall? Wasn't this this the man who was going to lead the Rams on to great things? The answers were 'possibly' and 'no'. As time passed, never was it more starkly illustrated that sports clubs need to have the decision-making processes of the business in the hands of people who know something about the business they are operating in. The 'Maxwell factor' began to hang like a shadow over the club. It infiltrated every nook and cranny. Derby prides itself on being a football town. Despite Maxwell's hectoring, attendances steadfastly refused to rise to the 20,000 he kept saying they needed to reach if he was to continue take an interest. The team finished 15th in Division One, but Wright made six appearances for England, including one as substitute. His international career was back on the road.

For the next two seasons Wright was voted Derby County's Player of the Year. As Arthur Cox said at the time of his transfer to Liverpool: "Well, Mark has everything you'd want a football player to have. He grew up an awful lot while he was here and there's virtually nothing on the football field that he can't do." Coming from the usually taciturn Cox, that is rare praise indeed.

Wright was tall, strong in the air, mobile over the ground and had good ball control. He was easily identified because of his gingerish hair and rather receding hairline and he could be impetuous, especially in his youth. Southampton supporters were known to hold their breath when Wright launched himself in his early days at The Dell. That ground is tight and 13½st of wild-eyed enthusiasm coming towards you can be intimidating. Wright also had some forceful opinions, which he wasn't behind the door at expressing sometimes and he fell out with England manager Bobby Robson after the 1988 European Championships in Germany. He returned for the 1990 World Cup in Italy, where he played outstandingly well and he won 24 of his 45 England caps whilst he was a Derby County player, during which time he undoubtedly matured and improved.

With Maxwell looking to get his money back, Derby County relegated and anxious to be rid of their suffocating benefactor, Wright was sold to Liverpool for £2.5 million in July 1991. He became club captain at Anfield and led them to an FA Cup Final victory. After retiring in 1998, he moved into management at Conference club Southport, with Ted McMinn as his assistant and then to Oxford United, where he began his career.

Ray Young – compared to a great player

IT must be hard for a player to be always compared to somebody else. Ray Young had that cross to bear, at least in his early career. Fortunately, in his case it was really a compliment, as the player he was most likened to was Leon Leuty and he was one of Derby County's best-ever centre- halves. Being compared to a poor player must be real hardship.

Young was born and bred in Derby. That, too, is not necessarily a good thing. 'Local boy makes good' headlines can be hard to handle. Many players have found the expectations of friends, relatives and acquaintances too immediate and demanding, but Young took all of it in his unhurried stride. If not quite the player that Leuty was, Ray Young had some of Leuty's easy style and Leuty had plenty of that to spare.

Managers of clubs in this country can be suspicious of style and Young found himself out of favour at various times of his career, being replaced by more pragmatic and prosaic performers. Nevertheless, he made 268 appearances, plus one as substitute, in a professional career that spanned 15 years at Derby County, which was his only club. One place he has occupied for a very long time. Nobody – style, or otherwise – has yet managed to displace him as the final name on Derby County's alphabetical lists.

Derby County won the first peacetime FA Cup Final in 1946 and Young grew up in the immediate post-war era, when Derby County were breaking British record transfer fees and bringing stars like Billy Steel and Johnny Morris to the Baseball Ground. By the early 1950s, however, the team was declining, which culminated in relegation to Division Two in 1953 and the Third Division North in 1955. It meant that although Young had joined the Rams, after playing for England Boys v Scotland Boys, in 1949 when all the trappings of a high-profile First Division club were still in evidence, he didn't make his debut until 1954 – he was 20 years old – and by then, the Rams were fading fast.

When Harry Storer succeeded Jack Barker as manager, Young quickly found himself in competition for the centre-half position with first Ken Oliver, then Martin McDonnell, and, finally, Les Moore. The latter two were, to put it mildly, rugged individuals with few inclinations about constructive play. Storer preferred defenders who tackled first, second and third and asked questions afterwards. Young quite often found himself making the trip up to the manager's office to find out exactly where he stood. He usually discovered that having been in there for half an hour, he was more confused when he came out, than he was when he went in. Many others had much the same experience. Nevertheless Young made about a third of the League appearances possible whilst Storer was manager. That ratio went up to half after Tim Ward arrived. He eventually gave way to Bobby Saxton in 1966.

These days he doesn't miss many games at Pride Park and has some sharp views on football past and present. Whatever might, or might not have been, regarding potential not quite fulfilled, few individuals have remained more loyal to Derby County than local boy, Ray Young.

Bibliography

Football Managers, Dennis Turner & Alex White, Breedon Books, 1993.

Football Players Records 1946-1984, Barry J Hugman, Newnes Books, 1984.

Steve Bloomer, Peter Seddon, Breedon Books, 1999.

The Derby County Story, Anton Rippon & Andrew Ward, Breedon Books, 1998.

Illustrated History of Football, Chris Nawrat & Steve Hutchins, Octopus Publishing Group, 1998.

Journeys with Jobey, Edward Giles, The Hallamshire Press, 2000.

Clough, The Autobiography, Brian Clough with John Sadler, Partridge Press, 1996.

The Kingswood Book of Football, ed Stephen Kelly, Kingswood Press, 1992.

The Who's Who of Derby County, Gerald Mortimer, Breedon Books, 1992.

A Strange Kind of Glory, Eamon Dunphy, William Heinemann Ltd, 1991.

Footballer's Progress, Raich Carter ed. E Lanchbury, Sporting Handbooks, 1950.

The Great Days of Derby County, ed Anton Rippon, Breedon Books, 1993.

Images of Derby County, Anton Rippon & Raymonds Photographers & Press Agency, Breedon Books, 1995.

Derby County Days, Edward Giles, Interleaf Productions Ltd, 1997.

Premier League Record File, Smith, Virgin Books, 2000.

The Footballers' Fireside Book, compl. Terence Delaney, William Heinemann, 1963.

Voices of The Rams, Ian Hall, Breedon Books, 2000.

History of English Football, Robert Jeffery with Mark Gonella, Paragon, 2000.

Derby County: A Complete Record 1884-1988, Gerald Mortimer, Breedon Books, 1988.

Journey Through a Season, Ian Hall, Breedon Books, 1997.

Fever Pitch, Nick Hornby, Victor Gollancz, 1992.

Arrivederci Swansea, Mario Risoli, Mainstream, 2000.